Liberty Style

Mervyn Levy

Liberty Style

The Classic Years: 1898/1910

RIZZOLI
NEW YORK

For Marion Selina

First published in the
United States of America in 1986 by
RIZZOLI INTERNATIONAL
PUBLICATIONS, INC.
597 Fifth Avenue, New York NY 10017

Library of Congress Cataloging-in-
Publication Data

Levy, Mervyn.
    Liberty Style

    Bibliography: p.
    Includes index.
    1. Liberty & Co.   2. Decoration and
ornament—
England—Art Nouveau.   I. Title.
NK1535.L67L48   1986   745.4′4942132
        85-43479
ISBN 0-8478-0697-9

Designed by Simon Bell

Typeset by Keyspools Ltd, Golborne, Lancs
Colour separations by Newsele Litho Ltd
Printed in Italy by LEGO, Vicenza

Frontispiece
Rare 18-carat gold and plique-à-jour
necklace set with opals, designed by
Archibald Knox and executed by Liberty & Co
c1900.

Contents

Acknowledgments

THE AUTHOR AND PUBLISHERS would like to express their appreciation to the many museums, institutions, art galleries and private individuals who have provided access to their collections, photographs and archives. They are particularly grateful to Arthur Stewart-Liberty for his Foreword and to Ken Wootten, Head of the Antiques Department at Liberty & Co. Also to the following: Elizabeth Aslin, Jean Hamilton, Shirley Bury and David Coachworth of the Victoria and Albert Museum; the Art Gallery and Museums and the Royal Pavilion, Brighton; the Hunterian Art Gallery, University of Glasgow; Hill House, Helensburgh; the William Morris Museum, Walthamstow; Brian Murray, Curator of the Cannon Hall Museum, Barnsley; the National Portrait Gallery, London; the City of Westminster Archives; the Museum of Modern Art, New York; Nick Nicholson and Hawkley Studio Associates Ltd; James Dixon and Sons Ltd; the Manx Museum, Isle of Man; the Royal Incorporation of Architects, Scotland; Mark Turner and Roberta de Jola, the Silver Studio Collection of the Middlesex Polytechnic (in 1967 Miss Mary Peerless, Rex Silver's stepdaughter, presented the contents of the Silver Studio of Design to the Hornsey College of Art, which is now part of the Middlesex Polytechnic); Christie's, London; Sotheby's, London; the Fine Art Society, London; Fischer Fine Art Ltd, London; Christine Woods, archivist, Arthur Sanderson & Sons Ltd; the Rev. E. T. Jones, Vicar of the Church of St Brynach, Nevern, Pembrokeshire; Dan Klein; Adrian Tilbrook; Stuart Durant; Dennis and Sue Ewen; Peter Godday; Joseph Fitton; George and Joan Holden; John Bignall; Keith and Sue Mead; the Charles Rennie Mackintosh Society, Glasgow; Kathleen Haseler; David Hughes; Tony Coakley; Richard Dennis; Ann Harrison, librarian, the Manx Museum, Isle of Man; Caroline Fox; Alison Adburgham; Sasha Uberti; Philippe Garner; Jesse and Laski Ltd, London; Michael John; Michael Bruce; Jackie Scott; Gordon House for photographs of Liberty silver and pewter in his collection; Debbie Godday for photographs of Liberty jewellery in her collection; my editor Wendy Dallas, who helped shape my *Liberty Style*. And especially to my wife, Marie, for her perceptive reading of my text and the many helpful suggestions she made.

Foreword

I AM VERY GLAD that it is Mervyn Levy who has written this book. He has about him a certain grace and erudition which I am certain were the attributes of many of the designers and craftsmen about whom he writes. These attributes were certainly applicable to some of the men who were responsible, in the early days of Liberty's, for making its reputation.

Mervyn Levy has written a scholarly and attractive book about the fascinating period of design between the high point of William Morris's career and the somewhat murkier waters of 'Art Nouveau'.

Many volumes have been written about William Morris and about 'Art Nouveau'. The period between is not so well covered, and this book is therefore very welcome. At a time when so many famous designers and craftsmen were at work, it is strange that in some parts of Europe this special look, particularly in furniture, metal and fabrics, came somehow or other to be known as the Liberty Style. Today, I find it flattering and sometimes embarrassing that this should have been so because, in the present commercial and business climate, when large shops are judged mostly on the amount of profit they make and rather less on the excellence of their merchandise, it is perhaps not so easy as it was in the 1890s for a shop to exist successfully on buying and selling the work of innovating designers, however desirable this may be.

Nevertheless, the influence of the period about which Mervyn Levy writes is still discernible in some of the remoter corners of Liberty's, and the fact that there are still people called Liberty involved in the running of the place will, I hope, lend a certain edge and vitality to the history related here.

A. I. Stewart-Liberty
Great Missenden, Bucks

Introduction

THE LAST QUARTER of the nineteenth century and the short, sharp spell of feverish creativity in Europe leading up to the First World War witnessed the most volatile and inventive reorientation of aesthetic attitudes. In the area of the visual arts especially, new idioms were emerging with ever increasing rapidity. Shifts in vision and style landslided across the face of nineteenth-century culture, disintegrating in a mishmash of feverish Romanticism (Rossetti), histrionic Symbolism (Moreau) and exotic Aestheticism (Wilde). By 1914 French Cubism, Italian Futurism and English Vorticism had broken the patterns of the established mores. European aesthetics had been irrevocably changed, and the wave that washed away many now exhausted idioms would closely affect the nature of the applied arts. In Paris in 1874 the first Impressionist Exhibition had led a revolt against the moribund academicism of France and England. Before 1900 Van Gogh had approached the threshold of a fierce Expressionism, and Gauguin had penetrated the heartland of Symbolism. Everywhere the edifice of naturalistic, romantic and symbolist figuration was crumbling. The close, analytical exploration of the nature of appearances which began with the Impressionists was concluded by way of Cézanne, the Cubists and the Purists. But as early as 1879 the remarkable designer Dr Christopher Dresser anticipated the nature of Cubism – and Purism – in much of his work for the Sheffield silversmiths James Dixon & Sons Ltd. To my knowledge, no history of Cubism has ever made reference to the work of Dr Dresser and its clear relationship to the new aesthetic vision.

The extent to which this new vision had its origins in the art of the designer rather than that of the painter is often overlooked. We have come to accept far too easily that the gradual evolution of modern decorative design – what is now loosely described as Art Deco (a term derived from the 1925 Paris Exhibition 'Les Arts Decoratifs et Industriels Modernes') – stemmed directly from an amalgam, a cross-breeding, of the Cubist-Futurist-Abstract idioms of painting and sculpture. The truth is otherwise. Running parallel with, but slightly ahead of the liberation of form in painting, was the liberation of form in architecture and applied design. I

Teapots and other designs by Christopher Dresser, 1879. The Cubist-Futurist revolution was still some thirty years away when Dresser designed these remarkable objects. Photograph from James Dixon & Sons Ltd *Costing Book of Dresser Designs*.

Dante Gabriel Rossetti (1828–82) in a self-portrait of 1870.

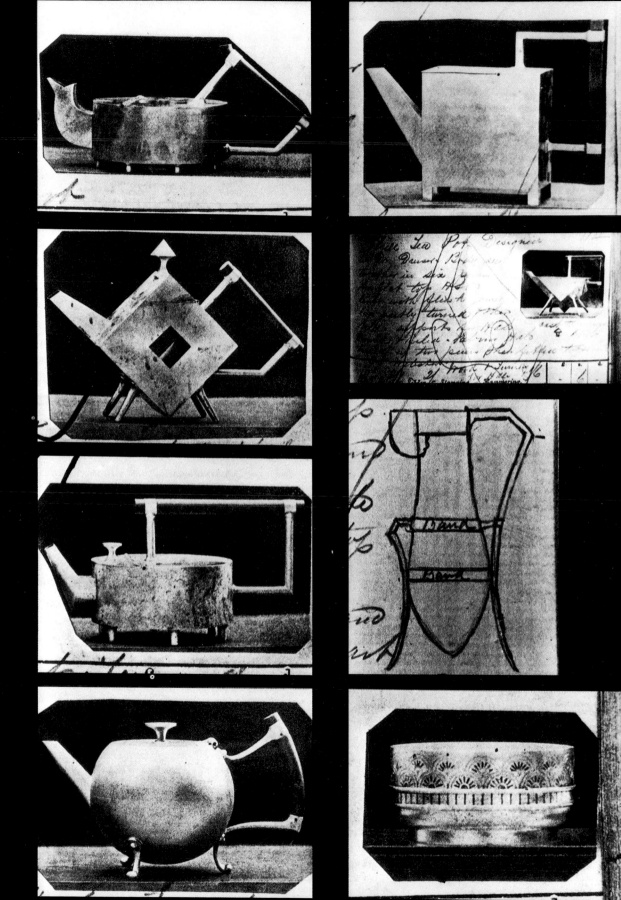

refer to a purity of form free from the need to pursue any loaded aesthetic or moral line, free especially from the need to express and reflect a high moral tone, as in the Neo-Gothic style, or any need to match the opulent requirements of the Victorian nouveau riche who wished to furnish their great houses with vulgar accessories. In painting, Cubism was heralded by Picasso's *Les Demoiselles d'Avignon*, painted during the winter of 1906–7. But the Vienna Secession was formed in 1897, and as early as 1900, in the eighth Secession Exhibition, there were contributions from designers C.R.Ashbee, Charles Rennie Mackintosh and Henry van der Velde.

Artists like Mackintosh, C.F.A.Voysey, Dresser and Archibald Knox (Arthur Liberty's key designer) were as important to the evolution and application of the new vision as were Picasso and Braque. The spirit of an age does not manifest itself in a solitary facet of activity. It reflects the need for change in a connected series of phenomena. Sometimes these may appear unrelated. But they are not. Only the narrow specialist can fail to relate the form-cleansing innovations of Knox and Picasso, or those of Mackintosh and the Purist painter Amédée Ozenfant. What all these artists reacted against was the flooding of the forms of art with the visual bilge of derelict aesthetic concepts. These were to be seen crowding the walls of the French and English Academies. True, there is at present a strong commercial revival of interest in the more brash and crudely literary academic painters of the late nineteenth and early twentieth centuries, an interest carefully sustained by the great sale rooms. But this is a matter of skilfully contrived fashion. The Liberty Style was one tributary of the cleansing river which by 1900 was radically altering the European aesthetic, in terms both of subject matter and the ideas behind it, and also in terms of the *form* of the artefact itself, whether this be a painting, a building, a piece of furniture or a pot. A Victorian building designed as an extension of Imperial grandeur – the Albert Memorial in London, let us say – had to encapsulate an essentially vulgar idea, and even a painting by the excellent Sargent, if he was commissioned to portray a brash or vulgar subject, suffered a corresponding debasement. But the idea which inspired an early Picasso Cubist painting or a design by Archibald Knox possessed in itself

Pewter vase *c*1903–4: a fundamentally simple design in which the spaces created by the arching of the arms are closely involved in the total conception. Height $13\frac{1}{4}$ in. Marked Tudric 0214.c.

a purity of conception which was correspondingly reflected in the clarity of its form.

It is revealing to note that Mies Van der Rohe described Mackintosh as 'a purifier in the field of architecture'. Certainly Mackintosh's clean design for the Glasgow School of Art (1897–1909) makes a refreshing contrast with the excesses of High Victorian architecture. What is remarkable is the extent to which Mackintosh, Dresser, Voysey – also an architect – and Knox were already underpinning the impending aesthetic revolution. In fact, one can say that before this revolution had taken place in the arena of the fine arts, it was well under way within its own terms of reference in French Art Nouveau, German Jugendstil and Stile Liberty, this latter being the term conferred by the Italians upon the Art Nouveau forms pioneered by Arthur Liberty – especially in the area of textiles – during the closing years of the nineteenth century and the opening decade of the twentieth century. It has since acquired 'generic' status.

Although this book is about the Liberty Style, in order to understand precisely what it was that the House of Liberty achieved during the period we are considering, it is of course essential to make comparisons, trace roots, and examine the context of the revolt in which it took part – for all innovatory art is a process of revolt against convention. The principal intention of this book is to demonstrate the nature of one such revolt.

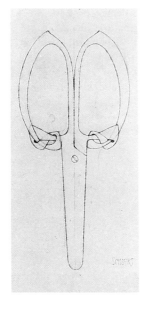

Overleaf Fabric design in watercolour by Archibald Knox, 1897–8, intended for Liberty & Co but never used. It contains the most radical, innovatory elements of the Liberty Style, notably strong geometric and abstract qualities which exerted a powerful influence on the work of Harry Napper, who also worked for the Silver Studio. It is now in the collection of the Manx Museum, Isle of Man.

Left Bannister in forged iron by Louis Majorelle, *c*1900. The wandering, fortuitous lines and rhythms of nature as exemplified by Majorelle were in complete contrast to the intellectual control of natural forms practised by such Liberty designers as Archibald Knox.

Above left Design for a pair of nail scissors by Archibald Knox, *c*1902. A brilliantly simple use of Celtic strapwork.

Left Tea and coffee service in pewter with cane-covered handles, designed by Archibald Knox. The low spherical and tall cylindrical shapes are decorated with a stylized honesty motif. Greatest height $8\frac{3}{4}$ in. width of tray 19 in. Rd. 420290. 023i. Design registered 1903.

Oak dining chair by C. F. A. Voysey, 1902,
with straight legs and leather upholstered
seat, the broad splat pierced with a simple
heart shape, a characteristic Voysey motif.
This chair was originally made by
F. C. Nielson who later produced a similar
chair in quantity. It may well have been
sold by Liberty in their Regent Street shop.
Liberty's documented association with
Voysey is tenuous, although their first
workshop supervisor, James Thallon, a
cabinet maker of Beak Street, Soho, was
himself responsible for the production of
many Voysey designs. It is likely therefore
that there was a cross-fertilization of style
through this intermediary.

Oak cabinet with bookshelves, c1900,
probably from Wyburd Studios. The style,
with its variously shaped cut-outs (especially
the heart shapes), owes something to the
influence of Voysey.

Music cabinet in mahogany with inlay of sycamore and other light-coloured woods, *c*1897. Possibly designed by C.F.A. Voysey. Lock stamped: Liberty & Co London.

Oak writing desk with brass mountings, designed in pure 'architectural' style by C.F.A. Voysey, who was himself an architect. Made in 1896 by W.H. Tingey. Probably sold by Liberty & Co.

Another fabric design in watercolour by Archibald Knox (see page 13), also produced for Liberty but not used. It too was executed in 1897–8 and its geometric abstract style was excitingly innovative.

The Evolution of the Liberty Style

FROM THE OUTSET Arthur Lasenby Liberty was a man apart. He brilliantly interpreted the taste of his time and catered for it meticulously. The style he created, with his pioneering team of designers, emerged from the turmoil of attitudes that prevailed in Britain in the last decade of the nineteenth century, when there coexisted the irreconcilable polarities of English aestheticism and French decadence, the philistinism of the merchant barons of industry who bought Tadema, Leighton and Poynter, and the purist searchings of designers Christopher Dresser, Charles Rennie Mackintosh and Archibald Knox. From these swirling cross-currents emerged a clarification of the forms of art that brushed aside both the exoticism of the aesthetes and the veiled eroticism of the decadents, and established an original and highly influential new form of artistic expression.

Many of the attitudes against which the Liberty Style reacted were embodied in the Aesthetic Movement, which was itself firmly rooted in two factors: the cult of Japonisme which invaded Europe in the wake of the International Exhibition of 1862, at which the arts and crafts of Japan were the main attraction; and the cult of personality which linked the passion for all things oriental and Japanese with the avant-garde. Its leaders in England were James McNeill Whistler and Oscar Wilde, who, in 1878, had swept upon the London scene in a dazzling flourish of wit and aesthetic ecstasy. Fresh from Oxford with the Newdigate Prize for Poetry, Wilde was the very quintessence of leisurely, foppish aestheticism. By the 1870s Japanese art in every form was readily available in the London stores, including Arthur Liberty's.

In practical terms Japonisme, combined with intellectual aestheticism, submerged the idea in the form, or rather in an amazing diversity of forms, for while the movement drew mainly upon Japanese art, it also borrowed extensively from the arts of Egypt, north Africa, Persia and China. A typical aesthetic interior of the period was awash with disparate styles, each tugging at its own very different source of inspiration. There was nothing homogeneous about such extravagant conglomerations. Though every item of furniture, pottery, porcelain, textile or carpeting was a work of art in

James McNeill Whistler (1834–1903) by Bernard Partridge, c1900. Whistler, a key figure in the Aesthetic Movement and a passionate Japoniste, was acquainted with Arthur Liberty as early as 1862–3, when he was buying Far Eastern items from Farmer & Rogers' Oriental Warehouse in Regent Street where Liberty was manager. In an interview years later Arthur Liberty said, 'Whistler always pretended that he valued my critical judgment, and certainly we had a feeling of sympathy on the Japanese Impressionist side of things . . . But no man, I suppose, was ever more independent of advice or less patient with it' (Alison Adburgham *Liberty's, A Biography of a Store*, page 28).

Oscar Wilde (1856–1900) in a photograph of 1884. The prince of aesthetes and one of Arthur Liberty's most distinguished friends, Wilde like Rossetti was fully aware of the new taste in fashion and fabrics created by Liberty & Co. 'I was determined', Arthur Liberty is reported as having said, 'not to follow existing fashions but to create new ones.' Asked if he had influenced Oscar Wilde he replied, 'Indeed, yes. My art fabrics were produced before he became celebrated. I gave him his opportunity and he helped me mightily with mine through the publicity he commanded.'

Dante Gabriel Rossetti with Theodore Watts-Dunton by T. Dunn, 1882. Rossetti, painter and poet, was a personal friend of Arthur Liberty and a frequent visitor to Regent Street to view and to buy the new fabrics of the day. The painting shows the artist (right) at home with his friend the writer Watts-Dunton in the typical, shapeless clutter of a late Victorian drawing room.

itself – the William de Morgan charger, the Christopher Dresser kettle on its stand, the drawings and paintings by Rossetti and Burne-Jones and the tiles by Walter Crane – the result was conflict. There was no harmony. The idea of interior design did not apply.

By the early 1880s society had divided itself into two camps: aesthetes and philistines. The concept of 'art for art's sake' was the lodestar of Camp One which stood firmly against any idea that art should have some moral, social or even political purpose. This would soon be hinted at by William Morris. The philistines in Camp Two eagerly swallowed the sentimentalities and fake historicism of Victorian narrative and neo-classical art. The strength of Camp One was sapped by the aimless and foppish posturing of the aesthetes, parodied widely in the journals of the day, and brilliantly in Gilbert and Sullivan's opera *Patience*:

> A Japanese young man,
> A blue and white young man,
> Francesca di Rimini, miminy piminy,
> Je-ne-sais-quoi young man!
>
> A pallid and thin young man,
> A haggard and lank young man,
> A greenery-yallery, Grosvenor Gallery,
> Foot-in-the-grave young man!

The Grosvenor Gallery had been the scene of the 1877 exhibition at which Whistler exhibited his painting *Nocturne in Black and Gold – the Falling Rocket*. The picture was attacked by Ruskin who accused the artist of 'flinging a pot of paint in the face of the public'. Whistler retaliated by suing Ruskin. The trial took place in 1878 and Whistler was awarded a farthing damages. The reference to 'greenery-yallery' relates to Liberty's Umritza Cashmere introduced by the firm in 1879 and described in *Queen* magazine as containing tints of 'green that look like curry . . .'

The 'blue and white' young man satirizes one of Wilde's favourite remarks that he was a young man whose greatest difficulty in life was living up to the level of his blue and white china. It was against this background of Japonisme, riotous aestheticism and humbug in Victorian narrative art that the Liberty Style evolved.

Born in 1843, the son of a Chesham draper, Arthur Liberty was a young man of thirty-three when, in 1875, he opened a small shop in Regent Street, London. Originally selling only ornaments and *objets d'art* from Japan and the East to cater for the current fashionable demand, he soon expanded to include fabrics, oriental carpets and china. William Morris, Alma Tadema, Burne-Jones, Rossetti, Whistler and Wilde were regular customers, which did much to consolidate Liberty's reputation with the fashionable cliques of the time. The greatest triumph of the company's early days was their dyed fabrics; silks in 'Liberty colours' were an influential element in the Aesthetic Movement, and the delicate pastel tints of blue, greenish-yellow, gold and coral became world famous.

Liberty was an impresario of genius, and his run with the hounds of Japonisme and the Aesthetic Movement was brief but brilliant. If it masked for a period his most fundamental contribution to the evolution of twentieth-century design, it was nonetheless of great significance. Writing in the catalogue of the Liberty Centenary Exhibition held at the Victoria and Albert Museum in 1975, Edmund Capon wrote: 'Liberty's contribution to the Japanese craze of the late nineteenth and early twentieth centuries, and its effect on decorative design, was fundamental . . .'

A man of great vision and imagination, Liberty catered for clients who were still caught up in the trappings of the Aesthetic Movement, but by the 1890s he began to sense the need for radical new dimensions. To provide for this need he employed a team of highly talented designers to create a distinctive and original style, an adventurous pursuit considering that the market was still largely Victorian in spirit.

Among this fresh talent was Archibald Knox, the ideal designer for Liberty. A Manx man, he was thoroughly versed in traditional forms of Celtic art – complex interlacings assimilated from the *Book of Kells*, and the decoration of Norse, Celtic and Manx crosses. Linked with his own highly personal imagination and the invention of new shapes and forms, these emblems provided the main sources of his inspiration in the design of silver and pewterware, and were to help to establish the basis of the Liberty Style.

Knox had arrived in London in the 1890s and first found employment in the design studios of Christopher Dresser at Barnes. Stuart Durant (lecturer at the Royal College of Art, and an authority on Dresser) suggests that Christopher Dresser, a close friend of Arthur Liberty, introduced the young man to the firm for whom he began designing silver in about 1899. Two superb examples of Knox's earliest work for Liberty are the silver buckle of 1899 (p. 26), one of the few pieces of their silver bearing a London hallmark, and the silver cup with cover carrying a Birmingham hallmark for 1900 (p. 27). As a designer of genius Knox ranks with any of his great contemporaries. What Mackintosh was to furniture, Knox was to the design of silver and pewter.

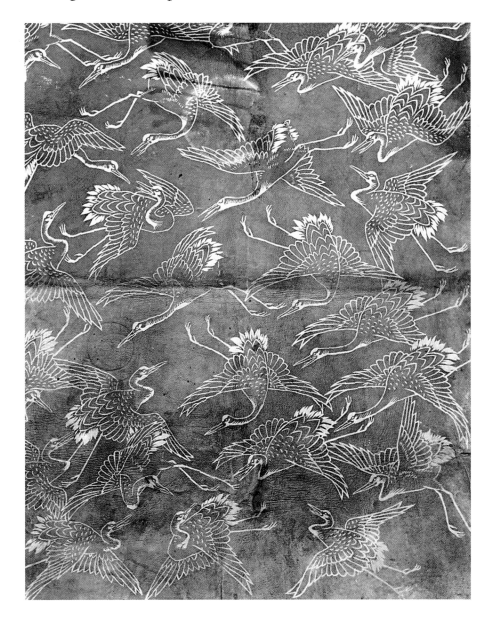

An example of Liberty's involvement in the craze of Japonisme: a three-foot length of stencilled leather from Japan (late nineteenth-century) believed to have been bought from Liberty's in the 1880s. The beautiful resist-dyed stencil design depicts cranes in flight, a symbol of longevity.

Copper log box with
repoussé lid set with a large
enamel medallion and
decorated with stylized
plant forms, c 1905.
Width 30 in, height 18 in.
Probably Wyburd
Studios.

Silver buckle with stylized
plant motifs, 3 in × 2 in.
Marked L & Co. Bears
the London date letter for
1899.

Silver cup and cover with blue and green
enamel decoration designed by Archibald
Knox c1899–1900. Height 11 in.
Birmingham town mark for 1900. Maker's
mark Liberty & Co, also stamped Cymric.

Photograph frame in silver and enamel designed by Archibald Knox. The conception is abstract, based on Celtic style interlacing with knots. Height 10 in. Bears Birmingham date letter for 1903. Marked L. & C, Cymric.

Inset in the frame is a photograph of Archibald Knox in middle age.

Above right Decorative Jugendstil dish in pewter by Württembergische Metallwarenfabrik (W.M.F) *c*1900. Width 15 in. A splendid example of the exotic and decadent High Jugendstil which so displeased Arthur Liberty.

Right Detail of Celtic knot motif from a Liberty & Co copper wall mirror, probably from a design by Archibald Knox, *c*1903. The design is a fine example of the stylization of a motif derived from Celtic sources but existing in its own right as an element of abstract design. Reverse carries ivorine label: Liberty & Co. London. W.

Top Green glass flower bowl by James Powell & Sons of Whitefriars, London, with pewter mounted with enamelled stylized plant forms probably designed by Archibald Knox, *c*1904–5. Width 9¾ in. Marked Tudric.

Above Pewter box with hammered lid decorated with an enamel painting of a young woman against a background of stylized trees, *c*1904–5. Representations of the human figure are rare in Liberty ware, and this formal pose bears little stylistic resemblance to French Art Nouveau or German Jugendstil. Length 4½ in. Marked with number only: 0386.

Three examples of Clutha glass *c*1904–5 and, on the right, an aubergine vase of Monart glass (mid-1920s), all set in pewter mounts probably designed by Archibald Knox. Height of tallest piece 9½ in.

Both Arthur Liberty and Archibald Knox were hostile to the voluptuousness of Continental Art Nouveau, with its powerful strain of decadent sexuality. Streams of hair moving in great swirling masses around the swooning faces of girls, or cascading in torrents about their undulating bodies, were distressing to the British taste. Not perhaps without cause: taken to extremes this vein of irritating eroticism led to a series of puerile images. Although at its best the sexuality of Jugendstil, with its luxuriant, thinly disguised hair fetishism (p. 29), matched perfectly the decadence of the 1890s, it was unacceptable to Arthur Liberty.

In the designs he commissioned the erotic image was banished, the vision cleansed. Decorative content was radically simplified and related to forms of a highly ingenious character, many of them loosely based on the prototypes of Celtic art, including Celtic jewellery of the ninth and tenth centuries that had been excavated in the nineteenth century. The human form, which had dominated the art of the Victorian age, was almost entirely absent from the main body of Liberty design. Occasionally it was to creep back in some unobtrusive, discreet form, as a feature in the enamel paintings that embellished the lids of pewter boxes and caskets (p. 30). But these more usually depicted landscape and river scenes or ships in full sail. Such devices possess little aesthetic merit (though they were popular and commercially successful) but often the clean, simple shapes of the boxes compensate for the inconsequential nature of the image.

An intrinsic feature of the Liberty Style was the decorative use of gemstones and enamelwork, and the facing of wall mirrors with repoussé copperwork, into which were often set plaques of turquoise enamel or rich blue Ruskin Pottery 'buttons'. Furniture was also set with copper panels and leaded lights of clear and stained glass. Both pewter and silver were ornamented with enamel, and many pieces such as bowls and vases were fitted with liners of deep green glass made by James Powell & Sons of Whitefriars, London, or Clutha glass (the word derives from the old Scottish for 'cloudy') which was made by James Couper & Sons of Glasgow. It is delicate, usually pale green, yellow or amber in colour, with variegated bubbles and streaks, and sometimes patches of aventurine, a

Tall goose-necked Clutha vase in pale green glass with pink striations. Designed by Christopher Dresser. Acid-etched 'Clutha' and 'Designed by C.D.' Height $14\frac{1}{2}$ in.

34

Chair by Charles Rennie Mackintosh 1904–5. Probably from Hous'hill, Glasgow. As with Hoffmann and Wyburd, decoration is incidental to form. The conception is essentially pure and mathematical. The relationship of the cube to the square and the rectangle is as subtle as the elements in an abstract painting by Piet Mondrian.

brownish glass with copper crystals first manufactured in Murano. Cups, vases and inkstands, clocks and candlesticks, figure prominently in the designs of Knox and are often enriched with enamel and gemstones.

The Scottish artist and illustrator Jessie M. King designed jewellery for Liberty's, as well as buckles, toilet sets, and a number of textile designs. This is the closest the firm came to any direct contact with the Scottish school, based in Glasgow and led by Mackintosh, although it is clear that there was cross-fertilization in some of the design motifs, such as the stylized rose which frequently appears in Scottish Art Nouveau and is often incorporated into the design of Liberty copper and pewter mirrors (p. 44).

The 1880s had also seen the emergence of the Arts and Crafts Movement, with William Morris at the helm, urging a return to medieval standards of craftsmanship and design in the teeth of the Industrial Revolution and the growth of the machine age. Earlier, the Pre-Raphaelite painters had argued along similar lines, preferring medievalism to industrialism.

The Arts and Crafts Movement stood in sharp contrast to all the tenets of Aestheticism. The cry was no longer 'art for art's sake' but 'art for work's sake' – for the sake of guilds and businesses properly organized and run with pragmatic intent.

There was the Century Guild, the first English Arts and Crafts Society founded by the architect Arthur Mackmurdo c1882, and C. R. Ashbee's Guild of Handicraft, established in 1882 as an excursion of his School of Handicraft, the idea being that here he would re-create the working conditions of the medieval guild. A passionate educationalist, Ashbee was to exercise a profound influence on the Colleges of Art. Unlike most of their colleagues in the Arts and Crafts Movement, both Ashbee and W. A. S. Benson, owner of the Hammersmith company of that name, fully accepted the viability of the machine. Indeed, Benson delighted in his factory's production of machine-turned metalwork. As *The Times* noted in their obituary of this distinguished architect, metalworker and designer:

'... he preferred to approach his subject as an engineer rather than a hand-worker; to produce his beautiful forms by machinery on a commercial scale rather than as single works of art ... His lamps, vases, entrée dishes, etc, were all the outcome of profound study of the capabilities of heavy stamping plant, spinning lathes and shaping tools which he was able to put down in his Hammersmith works ...'

(see Haseler's methods of production, pp. 92–119).

We now enter the age of the great art school principals: R. Lethaby at the Central School in London; Edward R. Taylor at Birmingham; Francis Newberry at Glasgow. There was the foundation of the Art Workers Guild in 1884, and the workmanlike simplicity of the furniture made by Ernest Gimson, Sidney Barnsley and C.F.A. Voysey. In his book *Homes, Sweet Homes* Osbert Lancaster ironically summarized the lifestyle of the Arts and Crafts Movement: 'Ever since the eighties in the byways of Chelsea and the lost valleys of the Cotswolds a handful of devoted Artists and Craftsmen had been living the simple life according to the doctrines of William Morris, surrounded by hand-woven linens, vegetable dyed, and plain unstained oak furniture by "goode workmen wel wrought".'

Clearly the Liberty Style has a rapport with the Arts and Crafts Movement, but it is in no way linked to any concept of medievalism, or to the first faint stirrings of modern Socialism which underlay the work and aspirations of William Morris. It was part of the awakening of the modern spirit in concert with the Scottish and Viennese Schools. And if it is to be argued that just as the artists of the Aesthetic Movement drew upon extraneous sources, so did Knox, the counter argument is plain. At no point did the Celtic idea weaken or destroy the purity of Knox's forms. Only a little later, in 1906–7, Picasso was to begin his long series of unashamed borrowings when he painted *Les Demoiselles d'Avignon*, clearly inspired by African art. But no matter what his sources of origin, the idea never disturbed the purity of the forms used by Picasso. This quality is what distinguishes the designs of Knox, and of his first mentor, Dr Christopher Dresser. The functionalism which marked Dresser's theories and which, in any final analysis of his significance, far superseded his early passion for Japonisme, inevitably influenced Liberty's designers.

Pablo Picasso *Les Demoiselles d'Avignon* (1906–7). This seminal Cubist painting belongs to the period when Christopher Dresser and Charles Rennie Mackintosh had already evolved their own geometric style and when the 'geometry' of the Liberty Style was in full flower.

Silver tea-set decorated with stylized Celtic knots. Designed by Archibald Knox and executed by Liberty & Co. Hallmarked 1903. Bowl 2 in; teapot 6 in; jug 1¾ in.

Silver and enamel mirror frame, probably designed by Archibald Knox. Repoussé with Celtic design incorporating flower-head motifs. Enamelled in blue, green, yellow and shades of orange. Height 18¾ in. Marked L & Co; Cymric; Birmingham date letter for 1902.

Arthur Liberty's awareness of the need for change derived partly, at least, from his close friendship with Christopher Dresser, whose son Louis joined the furnishing department at Liberty in 1896. Dr Dresser had himself managed a shop in New Bond Street in 1880 called Art Furnishers' Alliance, where he sold metalwork, furniture, glass and pottery, mostly worked from his own designs. He spoke and wrote widely of the significance of ornament in relation to the artefact, yet his most successful designs are those in which ornament plays no part. He recognized the importance of function, or 'fitness for purpose', arguing further the crucial point that 'all decorated objects should appear to be what they are; they should not pretend to be what they are not'. This prefigures in essence the basic philosophy of the Bauhaus, formed at Weimar in 1919 under the direction of the architect Walter Gropius. It was the first fully concerted attempt to reconcile design with the demands of machine production. In the catalogue of the Bauhaus Exhibition held at the Royal Academy in 1968 Ludwig Grote wrote: 'Functionalism became the creative principle of the Bauhaus . . . in order to create something that functions properly – a container, a chair, a house – its essence had to be explored for it should serve its purpose to perfection, i.e. it should function practically and should be durable, inexpensive and "beautiful".' Gropius had himself also spoken of the meaning of functionalism as the 'organic shaping of things dictated by the presence of their own law, without romantic palliation and playfulness'.

These are precisely the 'laws' acknowledged by Dresser in so many of his simple, unadorned designs. The basic forms of many Knox and other Liberty designs are also functional, easy to handle and to use, perhaps not always matching Dresser's achievements in this respect, but they clearly point out of the nineteenth and towards the twentieth century. The elements of 'romantic palliation and playfulness' are still present but, ornament apart, what form could be more purely and simply functional than the tea-set by Knox (pp. 94–5). And a great many of the vases, trays, baskets, bowls and a variety of other household objects by Liberty artists are equally practical.

Duplex-printed furnishing fabric titled 'The Beauly', probably designed by Jessie M. King c1910, with stylized trees, blue blossoms and pink ribbons.

Above Two pewter clocks. The one on the left, designed by Archibald Knox *c* 1903–4, has a face in blue-green enamel with central motif in red enamel, decorated with plant forms. Marked: English Pewter, Made by Liberty & Co. 0609, Rd No. 468016, Solkets. The other has a copper and enamel face in a pure, simple shape, *c* 1903. Height 9 in. Marked: Tudric 0371.

Right Green glass beaker by James Powell & Sons of Whitefriars, London, and pewter holder by Archibald Knox decorated with a pierced design of stylized leaves, berries and tendrils. Rd No. 460340 0534. Design registered in 1905.

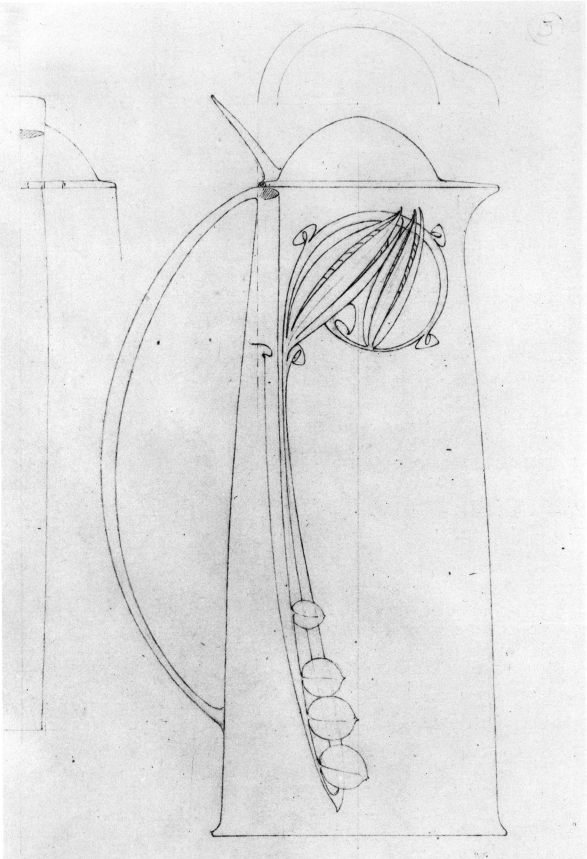

Opposite Design by
Archibald Knox for a hot-
water jug, *c* 1902.

Left Pewter jug with cane
handle designed by
Archibald Knox *c* 1902.
Marked Tudric only.

Left Detail from copper mirror surround with highly stylized green enamel rose and repoussé leaves on long stems. Probably Scottish School *c* 1905–6. The design is the standard stype of formalization typical of both the Scottish School and Stile Liberty at this period.

Right Brooch in silver and enamels by Jessie M. King, 1906, using an inventive stylization of birds and flowers set in space. Width $1\frac{5}{8}$ in. Marked Liberty & Co.

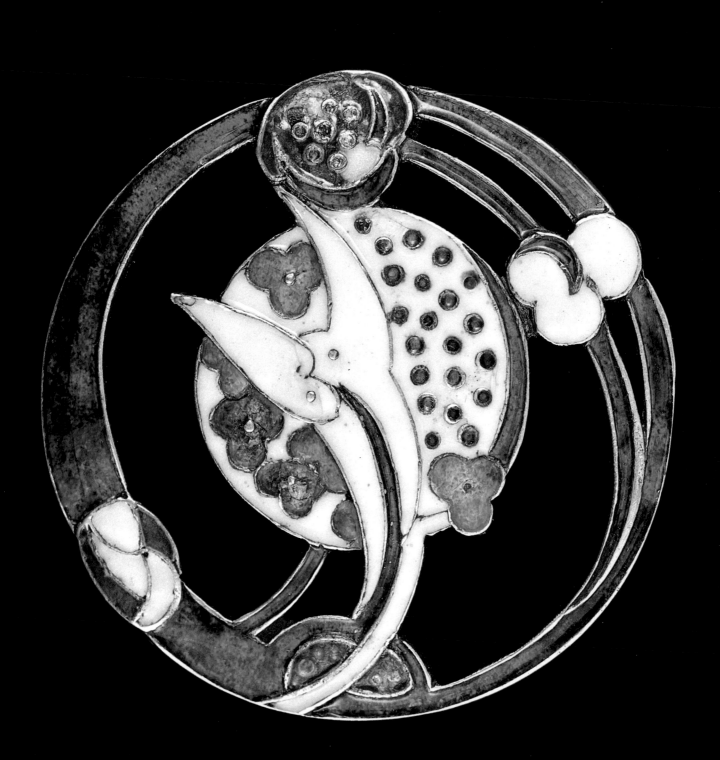

Claret jug mounted in silver, the thumb-piece holding a piece of lapis lazuli, probably designed by Archibald Knox. The green glass flask was made by James Powell of Whitefriars. Height 13 in. Marked L & Co, stamped Cymric, and bearing the Birmingham date letter for 1902.

Pair of turquoise-painted metal candlesticks with brass-plated mounts and wooden handles, designed by Christopher Dresser and made by Richard Perry & Co of Wolverhampton c 1883. Simplicity of form linked to function was the basic principle which underlay the revolutionary designs of Dr Dresser. Nowhere is a prefiguration of the Bauhaus concept more apparent than here. They were sold by Liberty & Co and described in their catalogues as the 'Kordofan' candlesticks in 'Liberty Art Colours'. Height $5\frac{3}{4}$ in.

Pewter tea service designed by Archibald
Knox, c1903. Length of tray 19½ in.
Marked Tudric.

At its best, Liberty produced the clearest responses to the need for change and, in the work of its main designers, an indication of the ultimate destiny of industrial design. It was an intrinsic part of the radical recasting of western aesthetics, pointing towards the decorative arts of the 1920s and related to contemporary abstract art. Stripped of their ornament, a great many of Knox's designs comprise simple geometric elements: circles, cylinders, cones, squares, pyramids, cubes and rectangles. And although the ornament draws its figurative inspiration mainly from Celtic sources, and from a stylized modification of plant forms, it is not difficult to discern the essence of that which Clive Bell described as 'significant form': purity of form irrespective of subject or its adornment. This presupposes that the idea must not dominate the form. Of course the subject – the idea – matters but it must not transcend, or act in conflict with, the form of the object.

The qualities that distinguish the Liberty Style apply whether one is considering a three-dimensional object – a clock, vase, table or teapot – or a two-dimensional one – a textile or wallpaper. In the former the purity and simplicity of the overall form is paramount, its decoration complementary. This subsidiary element should be unobtrusive yet contribute to a realization of the form of the object. If it is circular or square the decoration should stress the nature of the form. It must not, as in so much Victoriana, emerge from the form as an excrescence, existing in its own right. In the latter, the design of wallpapers and textiles, the move towards simple stylization is the keynote.

Below Pewter biscuit box decorated with two separated bands of abstracted geometric leaf motifs, the top band linked by interlacing tendrils. Probably designed by Archibald Knox, *c* 1902–3. Height 5½ in. Marked: Tudric. Made in England.

Below right Cylindrical pewter biscuit box decorated with square leaves and stylized flower forms set with blue-green enamels. Probably designed by Archibald Knox 1903–4. Height 5 in. Marked: Made for Liberty & Co. English Pewter 0193.

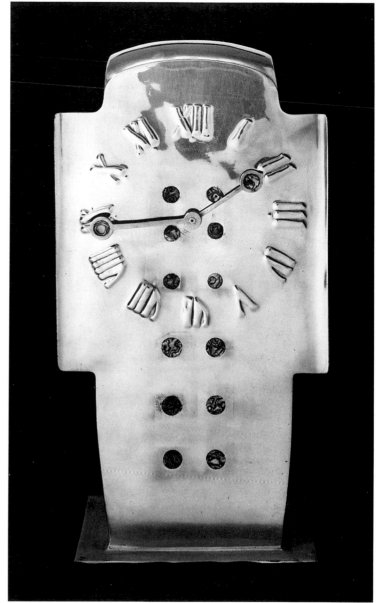

Pewter string box and cutter, c1902. Height 7½ in. Marked: Tudric, Hand Wrought Pewter, Liberty & Co 0172.

Pewter clock by Archibald Knox c1901-2, set with circular enamel motifs. The design is loosely based on an abstracted variation on the theme of the Celtic cross. Marked: Tudric.

Nowhere in the design of the period is this move more clearly realized than in the work of the architect Charles Francis Annesley Voysey (1857–1941). He produced many fabric and wallpaper designs for Liberty. Where Knox developed his unique stylization of plant motifs, Voysey's use of plant and especially bird motifs had heralded the stylized imagery of the 1920s as early as 1893 (see opposite). The catalogue of the Voysey Exhibition held at the Art Gallery and Museum, Brighton, from 1 July to 3 September 1978 refers to his use of bird motifs in the section on pattern design: 'The bird in all its variations became in effect the Voysey trademark ...' In the absence of records, it is a matter of conjecture as to whether certain designs by Voysey were in fact used by Liberty. Many designs are known to have been commissioned directly from the artist; others are less certain. The Stag design of 1896 (pp. 52–3) was originally designed as a wallpaper and subsequently woven by Alexander Morton & Co as a Liberty furnishing fabric. Some designs may have found their way to Liberty via the Silver Studio (see p. 77) with whom Voysey had close connections. This studio based a number of its products on wallpaper designs by the artist, usually incorporating one or other of his bird themes. One design by Voysey which may have been used by Liberty incorporates a typical sweep of birds (p. 55), closely related to those which appear in different formation in the Stag design. It is, in spirit and conception, characteristic of the Liberty Style. Indeed, in terms of wallpapers, textiles, and fabric design in particular, Voysey exerted a profound influence on the evolution of that style, as he did on the designs of the Silver Studio where his work was greatly admired, notably by Harry Silver. He was also a furniture designer of great originality.

The purification of form by Knox was matched by the cleansing of two-dimensional design by Voysey. That many of their designs precede the year 1898 is an important pointer to the fact that there was a period of radical experiment before the final emergence of a fresh aesthetic direction.

*　　　*　　　*　　　*

C.F.A. Voysey (1857–1941) in a drawing by Harold Speed, 1896.

A watercolour of 'Seagulls' designed by C.F.A. Voysey c1890–1. Produced as a double-cloth by Alexander Morton & Co 1897–8 and probably sold by Liberty & Co.

52

Woollen double-cloth designed by
C.F.A. Voysey: a landscape repeat with
stags and birds, predominantly in blue
and green with pink outlines and details.
Woven for Liberty by Alexander
Morton & Co c1897.

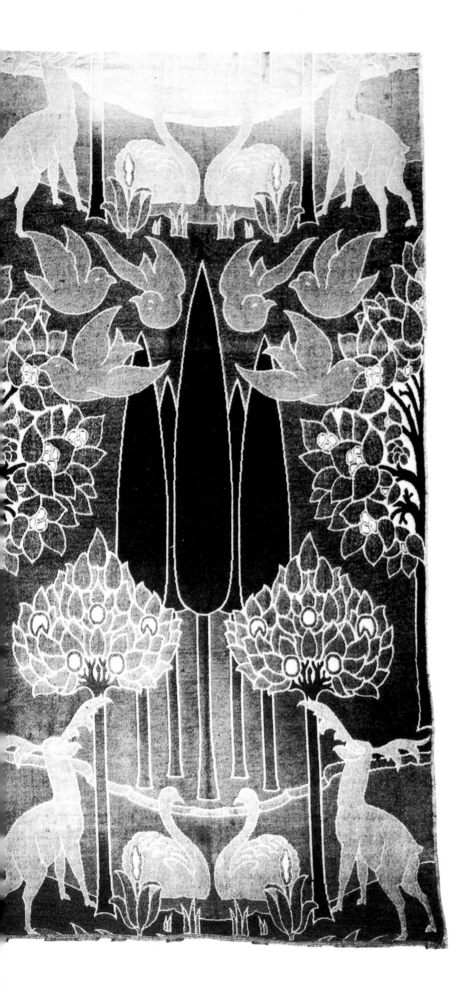

Wool tapestry designed by
C.F.A. Voysey, 1893.
Woven by Alexander
Morton & Co and
probably sold by Liberty
& Co.

Design for wallpaper entitled 'Isis' by C.F.A. Voysey c1893,
using characteristic stylization of bird, plant and flower motifs.
Produced by Jeffrey & Co and probably sold by Liberty's.

Top Small pewter cake tray *c* 1904, probably
designed by Archibald Knox. It has gently
curving sides and an oval centre, and is
decorated with stylized leaves and flowers.
Marked: English Pewter, 0547.

Above Pewter cake basket decorated with
stylized square leaves on trailing stems.
Probably designed by Archibald Knox,
c 1905. Length 12 in. Marked: Tudric 0357,
Rd. 449032 (design registered in 1905).

Generally speaking, I use the term Liberty Style not only to describe innovations for which the company was responsible but also to show the influence of their pioneering work on numerous other designers and manufacturers of the period. Furniture makers were particularly prone to copy and pastiche the designs of Leonard F. Wyburd, whose Furnishing and Decoration Studios were officially established in Regent Street, London, in 1883. He provided Liberty with much of the furniture they sold, and his work prompted the *Cabinet and Art Furnisher* to list Liberty & Co as one of the 'high class firms' associated with furniture.

The Thebes Stool, mahogany; also made in oak. The design was patented by Liberty in 1884, the year after the opening of their Furnishing and Decoration Studios. It was described in the firm's catalogue as a 'reproduction of an ancient Egyptian model'. Another version had four legs and a concave, thonged leather seat. These stools were among the first products to come from Leonard Wyburd's new studios, and this particular one was sold extensively throughout Europe and was stocked by Samuel Bing in his Paris shop, La Maison de l'Art Nouveau, which he opened in November 1895. Its origins apart, the simplicity and 'originality' of its shape well matched the evolving avant-garde mood of Wyburd's studios.

The bedroom suite that was made for a Liberty client in 1904 is an example of the originality and quality of the work produced by his studios. Wyburd's furniture led the way to a more radical approach in modern applied design. The geometric idiom of the 1920s is foreshadowed by the washstand/chair (p. 63) which was probably designed by Leonard Wyburd in 1899. The straight line, the square and the circle are the basic elements in its extraordinary design, which anticipates, even beyond Cubism, the pure relationship of the square and the circle in the abstract art of Ben Nicholson.

Designs for room settings, interior decoration and textiles, as well as furniture and its fitments — locks, handles, hinges — and such pieces as the fire basket of 1900 (pp. 60–1) all emanated from the Wyburd Studios.

They used predominantly oak in the manufacture of furniture for Liberty, with some solid walnut (polished), golden ash, mahogany and maple. For marquetry inlay — in which Wyburd specialized — a variety of fruit woods were also used, such as pear and apple, which are close-grained and easily cut into small, thin sections.

Two chairs and matching occasional table in walnut, decorated with mother-of-pearl inlay and fruit woods, c 1900, Wyburd Studios. Height of chairs 40 in, height of table 26 in.

Oak wardrobe from a specially
commissioned bedroom suite. Wyburd
Studios *c* 1904. Its simple geometric design
incorporates marquetry panels of stylized
peacocks in pewter and ebonized and
stained fruit wood. Brass fittings.

Design for a fire basket, with the certificate of its patented registration, 1900: an interesting example of the kind of simple, functional item produced by Liberty & Co in their Furnishing and Decoration Studios.

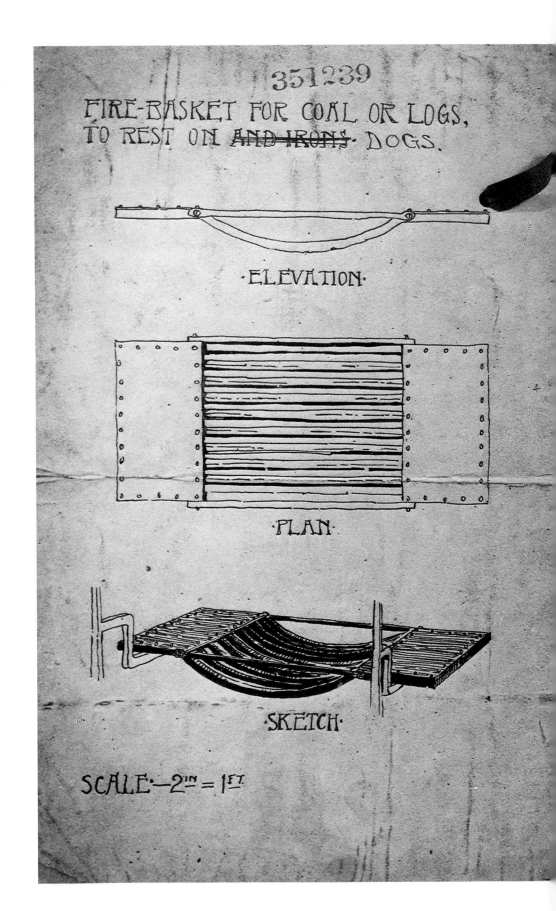

PATENTS, DESIGNS, AND TRADE MARKS ACTS, 1883 to 1888.

Certificate of Registration of Design.

R⁴. No. 351239

THE PATENT OFFICE: DESIGNS BRANCH,

25, SOUTHAMPTON BUILDINGS,

CHANCERY LANE, LONDON, W.C.,

1900.

This is to certify that the Design, of which annexed is a Copy, was registered this *2nd* day of *January* 1900, in respect of the application of such Design to articles comprised in Class *One* in pursuance and subject to the provisions of the Patents, Designs, and Trade Marks Acts, 1883 to 1888.

C. N. DALTON.

Liberty & Co. Ltd

EXTRACT FROM DESIGNS RULES, 1893.

Rule 5.—For Rule 32 of the Designs Rules, 1890, shall be substituted the following Rule:—

32. Before delivery on sale of any article to which a registered design has been applied, the proprietor of such design shall if such article is included in Class 13 or Class 14 in the Third Schedule hereto cause each such article to be marked with the abbreviation Regd., and shall, if such article is included in any of the Classes 1 to 12 in the Third Schedule hereto, cause each such article to be marked with the abbreviation Rd., and also, in the case of articles other than lace, with the number appearing on the certificate of registration.

W B & L (55o)—22961—10000-11-99

Oak washstand/chair from bedroom suite, probably designed by Leonard Wyburd at the Liberty Furnishing and Decoration Studios *c*1899. The woven straw back, thonged with leather, has a stencilled design, the top of the frame is inlaid with three stylized pewter flower forms and the cover is pewter. Its basic geometric conception shows signs of Egyptian influence.

Marquetry inset, in stained fruit woods with pewter moon, from the bedpost of the bedroom suite made by Liberty & Co in 1904.

Oak washstand from a bedroom suite
*c*1904, Wyburd Studios. It has marquetry
inlay of stylized fish in stained fruit woods
and pewter, with brass fittings.

Oak dressing table inlaid with pewter.
Pegged wood construction. Part of a
bedroom suite (see washstand p. 62)
probably designed by Leonard Wyburd
and made in Liberty's workshops *c*1899.
Height 5 ft 3 in.

BED · ROOM · FURNITURE · Etc. FROM · SPECIMEN · PAGE · IN
"LIBERTY" · HANDBOOK. · PART III.

Above Page from a Liberty
catalogue of 1890. The
furniture represented in this
drawing illustrates the
evolving simplicity of
Liberty design.

Ken Wootten, head of the Antiques Department at Liberty's, outlined for me not only the woods used most often in Liberty furniture but also the technique employed in the making of inlays, and the ways in which these little insets into the main, often plain, body of pieces of furniture could be made more ornamental. The introduction of ebonized woods, mother-of-pearl, bird's-eye maple and pewter added notes of striking decorative interest (p. 63), and in addition veneers were often stained from light to rich darks, and scorched by the sprinkling and sifting of hot sand over the surface of the wood.

A group of hitherto unpublished drawings from the Wyburd Studios, recently discovered at Liberty & Co, shows how clearly and categorically Liberty established a series of prototypes that provided the model for so much furniture that passes today as 'Liberty Style' (left and below).

Left A photograph *c*1901 recently discovered at Liberty & Co. The written documentation is fascinating, while the sideboard is a hitherto unrecorded example of the kind of furniture produced by a variety of hands at work in the Liberty Furnishing and Decoration Studios at this time. The large stylized heart-shaped hinges and the curious side-lamps are combined with a strong, crisp, geometric simplicity of form. The repoussé copper charger surmounting the sideboard is reproduced on page 149.

Above A recently discovered sheet of working drawings dating from about 1900 and emanating from the Leonard F. Wyburd Furnishing and Decoration Studios at Liberty & Co.

The early years of the furniture department at Liberty & Co are not well documented. We do know that silks, carpets, pottery, bronzes, porcelain and Japanese prints were imported, and the only domestic furniture made at home was small lacquered pieces, and octagonal Moorish coffee tables. There was, even in these early days, an Anglo-Arabian hall dressed with curtains, divan covers and fabrics of eastern origin. In 1880 the goods in the shop were departmentalized for the first time, and the new system included a furniture department. Soon furniture was available at 218 Regent Street as well as being displayed in premises at 42 King Street.

It was not until 1905 that Liberty became known as furniture makers in their own right, as distinct from suppliers, and it seems likely from what

Armchair in mahogany inlaid with stylized flower motifs in fruit woods, *c* 1900, reflecting the influence of C. F. A. Voysey. Height 5 ft. Probably Wyburd Studios.

Right Oak sideboard, probably designed by Leonard Wyburd and made in the Liberty Workshops *c* 1894–5. This piece of furniture contains all the features of the evolving Liberty Style in its sharp, clean geometric conception, though it is elaborately decorated with locks, handles and hinges and with a characteristic carved motto, repoussé copper panels (possibly by John Pearson) and candle-holders. The leaded lights are also in the geometric style.

Right Oak occasional table, Wyburd Studios *c* 1901–2. A strong geometric conception displaying sharp contrasts of the curved and the straight.

evidence survives that the working drawings for their designs were produced at the Liberty Studios in Regent Street and the furniture made up in small workshops in Soho and its environs by independent craftsmen, after which Liberty labels were affixed to the finished products.

In 1912 a fully fledged cabinet works was established at Highgate under the supervision of Albert Pannell, and this continued until its closure in 1940. Fabrics and textiles were, of course, produced by a variety of manufacturers, or at Merton Abbey from 1904, when Liberty & Co took over E. Littler's print works. They continued to hand-print there until 1973.

*   *   *   *

FIG. 1.—LIQUEUR SET AND TRAY, WITH FLORAL ORNAMENT IN LOW RELIEF (MODERN GERMAN.)

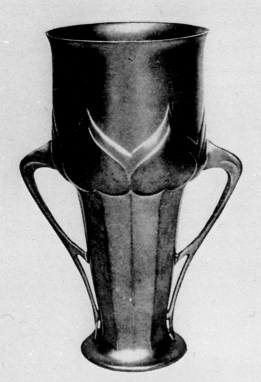

FIG. 2.—TWO-HANDLED VASE. (MODERN GERMAN.)

FIG. 3.—HOT-WATER JUG, WITH ORNAMENT IN LOW RELIEF. (MODERN ENGLISH.)

In 1899 Arthur Liberty had begun to import modern pewter from Germany into his Regent Street shop. His sale catalogues referred to these imports as 'Novelties in Pewter Ware'. They were manufactured mainly by the firms of J. P. Kayser & Sons of Krefeld (p. 108), Walter Scherf & Co of Nuremberg and L. Lichtinger of Munich. David Coachworth wrote in the catalogue of the Victoria & Albert Museum Centenary Exhibition of 1975: 'These firms were foremost in the revival of pewter production which had started in France and spread to Germany in the last decade of the nineteenth century. The quality of the metal was particularly appropriate to the swirling forms associated with Art Nouveau design and being less costly than silver, it made possible a range of decorative objects which would be available to a wider, less wealthy public. The success of these imported items in the English market must have influenced Liberty in his decision to restart the manufacture of pewter in this country.' And of course it must have prompted him to make a radical reappraisal of the kind of pewter design he wished to manufacture. Liberty were also selling at this time the pewter ware of Württembergische Metallwarenfabrik (W.M.F.) and other Continental pewter such as *Orivit* from Germany. In their metal foundry at Geislingen, some thirty miles south of Stuttgart, the manufacturers of W.M.F. produced a range of pewter which crystallized the essential character of High Jugendstil. On 17 May 1904 Arthur Liberty read a paper to the Society of Arts entitled 'Pewter and the revival of its use'. In this he spoke of the decline of pewter production in England, and of his recent revival of the pewter industry. He illustrated his paper by comparing items of contemporary German pewter with pieces of his new English pewter and noted pointedly that *his* pewter was decorated only with variations on the theme of Celtic forms, supported by plant and floral motifs. And he attacked the 'fantastic motif which it pleases our Continental friends to worship as "l'art nouveau"'.

At the personal instigation of Arthur Liberty, the company made its first tentative forays into the silver trade in the mid-1890s. A number of small firms in Soho seem to have made silver and jewellery for them in the early days, but when the venture really gathered strength around 1899 the

Page from a Liberty report of 1904 which compares 'modern' German pewter of advanced design with 'modern' English pewter. The German pewter is by J. P. Kayser & Sons and the Liberty hot-water jug from a design by Archibald Knox (see p. 43). All these items were sold by Liberty & Co.

main bulk of the manufacture was transferred to W.H.Haseler in Birmingham (see pp. 92–119). Some designs were then produced for them by local Birmingham artists – Arthur and Georgie Gaskin, Bernard Cuzner and Oliver Baker – but more often than not the identity of the designers commissioned by Liberty cannot be established. Their names were never given in the catalogues, and only appear in journals such as *The Studio*. The image Arthur Liberty wished to establish was that of his company rather than that of individual designers, and he neither encouraged nor indeed permitted them to sign or impress their work with any distinguishing mark. Attribution of individual pieces is often difficult for this reason. It is known, however, that a few artists, such as Knox, Oliver Baker and Bernard Cuzner, sold their designs direct to the company; in other cases attributions can safely be made on the grounds of style, though even a commissioned design was not necessarily used in its original form. Like all silver and jewellery firms, Liberty often had the original conceptions altered or redrawn (one such 'tracing book' still survives). And designs were adapted over the years and could be provided with variations to suit particular tastes. Therefore, when a design is described as 'probably after' any particular artist, this may be to allow for several intermediate transformations having taken place, or for the fact that it may even be a skilfully executed pastiche.

There is no doubt, on the other hand, that Liberty & Co chose their designers well, and that the silver they produced was exceptionally well made, generally living up to the claim of the 1900 illustrated catalogue that 'it possesses the soft natural sheen of the metal untouched, the desirable charm of variety being obtained by persistent originality of form and by the fact that all the work is hand-hammered. This it is, indeed, which secures that individuality which is so attractive, and which is an essential condition to secure the production of a real work of art.'

*   *   *   *

Poster for Job cigarettes by Alphonse Mucha (1860–1939), Paris, 1896–7. Although Mucha was an artist closely related to the contemporary spirit of decadence, his method of stylizing the rhythms, movement and flow of hair was more in line with Archibald Knox's geometric distillation of Celtic ornament than the erotic fetishism of Jugendstil and French Art Nouveau, with its emphasis on the sexuality of hair.

The problem of identifying the work of individual designers is encountered frequently in attempting to attribute decorative elements such as the copper panels that were often set into sideboards, chests and other items of furniture. There is no record of the names of the designers who produced them, although it is now clear that the coppersmith and ceramics painter John Pearson was one of the artists employed by Liberty. The Pearson story is an interesting one, though shrouded in some mystery. Such work as he signed is strikingly individual in character. It fits the simplicity of the Liberty Style only as an occasional note of complementary fantasy. It is a whimsical decorative flourish, a chord of indulgent vibrancy. It frequently

Newlyn chest, probably designed by John Pearson, with copper repoussé panels of galleons, fish, shells, seaweeds and dragons, c1898–9. Length 38 in. height 24 in.

reflects the passion of such contemporary potters as William de Morgan, the Martin Brothers and C.H.Brannam for grotesque creatures. Even so, it is entirely unique and personal to his own imagination. Having taught at C.R.Ashbee's Guild of Handicrafts (see Pearson entry, page 149), he worked for William Morris and other firms including the Newlyn Class, a group of Cornish copperworkers based in Penzance; certainly he was with them from about 1892. Until lately little was known of the group, but recent research by Caroline Fox of the City Museum and Art Gallery at Bristol has revealed a number of hitherto unrecorded details. According to Mrs Fox, 'John Pearson, a metal beater from Whitechapel came down to teach the teachers . . .' What Pearson must have taught them about the craft and technique of copper repoussé work seems to have been balanced by the range of local aquatic imagery he was to build into his own iconography: dolphins, crabs, squid, fish, shells and galleons were the stock images of the Newlyn Class. One piece of work which seems undoubtedly to have come from the hand of Pearson is the copperwork which appears as decoration around the fireplace of the room designed by Liberty & Co for Houghton Hall, Norfolk, in about 1909–10 (p. 76). Here the chief motifs of the design are variations on the theme of the dolphin rendered in the typically eccentric style of the artist. It may be assumed that after leaving the Guild of Handicrafts in 1892 Pearson went to work in Penzance, returning to London in the late 1890s to work occasionally for Liberty around and after the turn of the century. As Ken Wootten so perceptively concludes, it would have been inevitable in those days for a designer and craftsman as distinguished as John Pearson, operating in such a relatively narrow circle of specialists, to have found his way to Liberty's Regent Street shop. He is mentioned here, along with the Newlyn Group, because it now seems certain that Pearson, and through him the Newlyn school of copper-workers, played their part in establishing something of the iconographic content of Liberty copper products, along with handing on the technique of repoussé copper beating of which Pearson was a master.

*   *   *   *

Traditional room designed by Liberty &
Co c1909–10 at Houghton Hall, Norfolk.
Repoussé copper ornamentation of boats
and sea creatures around the fireplace
probably by John Pearson.

Liberty's policy of maintaining the anonymity of their designers is linked with a matter of some importance concerning a name closely associated with the design of Liberty metalwork: that of Rex Silver. Rex, the elder son of Arthur Silver who founded the Silver Studio in 1880, administered the Studio from 1901 until its closure in 1963, for the first fifteen years in partnership with his brother Harry.

In 1975, in the catalogue for the Liberty Centenary Exhibition, Shirley Bury of the Victoria and Albert Museum's Department of Silver was quite categorical in attributing a number of designs to Rex Silver; for example, the celebrated 'Conister' candlesticks of 1899–1900 (p. 79), which she describes as showing 'great verve'. However, Mark Turner in his introduction to the catalogue of the Silver Studio Exhibition held at the Museum of London in 1981 strongly expressed the opinion – subsequently and cautiously revised – that Rex Silver was too involved in the day-to-day running of the studio to have had any time for practical design work. On p. 101 of that catalogue he writes:

> Rex Silver had personally informed Mrs Bury that he was responsible for much of Liberty's metalwork. This was shortly before his death and he may well have been confused, for even then it was known that a considerable number of people outside the Silver Studio had designed for Liberty metalwork. Before the designs in the collection were discovered the only evidence of Rex's involvement in the Liberty metalwork venture was an illustration of a candlestick, the Conister, in *The Studio* magazine of 1900 (Vol XIX, p. 127). In fact this attribution to Rex is meaningless as we now know that Arthur and Rex *never* credited individual studio designers in any public mention of Silver Studio work ...

He also comments on Rex's administrative involvement with the Studio:

> We know from his [Rex's] surviving diaries that this was a more than full-time job ... It therefore seems even more unlikely

that he had the time to design metalwork for Liberty's over the period 1898–1905, when he would also be learning how to administer the Studio . . .

Whatever the truth, Mark Turner has now slightly modified his original views. In an interview he gave me at the Middlesex Polytechnic on 8 August 1985 he not only showed me a number of metalwork designs bearing detailed working notes in the hand of Rex Silver (the drawings themselves could have been by any member of the Studio design staff at the turn of the century), but said:

> We now know that Rex Silver did a few textile and wallpaper designs between 1912 and 1963. These are recorded in the Silver Studio Day Books. However, no early metalwork designs were recorded in the Day Books. But given the complexity of the working notes which are included with the designs, we know, since they are in Rex Silver's hand, that his involvement in metalwork designing as well must have been great. It is possible that some of the Liberty metalwork designs are by Rex himself – but many may have been a collaboration between Knox and Rex.

In any event, Rex was greatly influenced by Knox, who was in every sense the presiding genius and creative originator of the Liberty Celtic schemes (silver, pewter and jewellery), and the question of whether Rex Silver did produce any metalwork designs for Liberty must, it now seems, remain an open issue.

*   *   *   *

The 'Conister' silver candlesticks. Silver Studio *c*1899–1900. Applied struts on the columns separate at the top into stylized leaf forms below wavy drip pans. Detachable nozzles. The large, flat bases are expressive of the dramatic revolution in design which was rapidly transforming the whole concept of the applied arts. Since no candlesticks were included in the first exhibition of Cymric silver held in May 1899, this design must date from later that year or early the following year. The candlesticks were not however produced until 1906. Maker's mark: L & Co.

One of the greatest formative influences on the development of the Liberty Style was unquestionably Arthur Liberty himself, with his brilliantly imaginative realization that the impetus of organic Continental Art Nouveau was running out, and, at exactly the right time, of the need for change. He lived in close contact with the personalities of the period, tolerating rather than approving of either their art or their lifestyle, and he was, like all great impresarios, both of his time and a good way ahead of it. Arthur Harker's portrait (opposite) depicts a man who, while well able to make whatever 'friends' he chose, still remained aloof, detached and clearly determined to pursue and realize his own ideas. The narrowing eyes reflect more than a glint of the tough commercialism that established such a successful business, as well as a keen awareness of the aesthetic sensibility that produced the great era of Liberty design innovations.

That the need for aesthetic change should have been assessed with such foresight, first by Dresser and then by the emergence of the Liberty Style, establishes the origins – at least in spirit – of the Cubist-Futurist-Abstract stream as being of British rather than of French or Italian origin.

Perhaps it would be accurate to see the Liberty Style as a watershed linking what remained of the nineteenth-century need for pure ornamentation in design with the more rigorous dictates of the machine age – the point at which decoration would cease to exist as a cosmetic element and assume a more integral role, following the rules of shape and form, rather than fulfilling the function of eye-shadow or lipstick. William de Morgan, who supplied tiles to Liberty, and William Morris (though he is not on record as having designed for the firm), epitomize the ascendancy of ornament. By contrast, in many of their designs for furniture, Liberty moved with one firm step into the twentieth century. Here it was the ascendancy of shape and form which was the controlling force.

At the turn of the nineteenth century pure ornament was rejected by the mainstream of applied design in favour of a gradual acceptance of the significance and superiority of form – form, moreover, shortly to be closely linked with the machine. The machine-turning of the Bauhaus had not yet arrived, but the stage was set. The cleansing of form which began with

Sir Arthur Lasenby Liberty by Arthur
Hacker R.A. (1858–1919). Signed and
dated 1913.

The 'Wiclif' chair, in oak with rush seat, *c*1899. Its powerful geometric design is attributed to Leonard F. Wyburd. Liberty Furnishing and Decoration Studios. Height 40 in.

Christopher Dresser was completed by the Bauhaus, but only after its passage through the products of Liberty & Co and those of the Wiener Werkstatte (literally Viennese Workshops). Shortly before the founding of this workshop in 1903, Mackintosh had advised: 'Every object that leaves your hand must carry the outspoken mark of individuality, beauty, and most *exact execution*. . . . Begin today! If I was in Vienna I would help with a big, strong shovel!' This is clearly a critical reference to the dead hand of historicism, with its massive encrustations of ornament. The importance of

The bed recess in the master bedroom at
Hillhouse, Helensburgh.

The drawing room at Hillhouse, Helensburgh, designed by Charles Rennie Mackintosh, 1903. Mackintosh was a pioneer in the use of space as an integral element in the organization of interior design, and Liberty & Co were innovators in the purification of three-dimensional form and its decoration. Both streams were complementary aspects of the revolution in applied design which had begun to emerge as early as 1879 in the art of Christopher Dresser.

individuality and beauty was rightly stressed by the Wiener Werkstatte, but so was the reference to exact execution, a process which could only be completed by the machine. This ethic was not a marked influence as yet in the work either of Mackintosh or Liberty, but was certainly in evidence at times in the products of Dresser and Hoffmann. A brochure of 1905 explained that the Wiener Werkstatte was founded as an alternative to mass production by machinery. Josef Hoffmann who, more than any other Werkstatte designer, epitomized the spirit of reconciliation between the artist and the machine, began designing for machine production with a flare for purism which reflects and extends Mackintosh's concept of 'exact execution'. For there could be no such pattern of execution if the forms of art, their 'individuality and beauty' apart, continued to pay lip service to the tenets of the past. Writing in *Das Interieur II* in 1901, Hoffmann

Clutha vase in streaky green glass with bubbles and gold aventurine inclusions. Designed by Christopher Dresser and made by James Couper & Sons of Glasgow, c 1900. Height 13½ in. Sold by Liberty & Co.

Clutha glass vase with bent neck in yellow, green and red glass with silver aventurine inclusions. Designed by Christopher Dresser and made by James Couper & Sons of Glasgow, c 1895. Height 19½ in. Sold by Liberty & Co. Marked: Clutha. Designed by C.D. Registered mark encircling a butterfly.

argued: 'How can we create a new tradition if we cannot find followers in this poorest period of all time! We should start again at the very point where personal creativity had come to an end. Have we missed this possibility already? Didn't we have the same predecessors as they had in England?'

Hoffmann was arguing the case for a clean slate. The process of cleansing which he pursued, with its acknowledged debt to Mackintosh, must also have responded to the products of Liberty & Co, for although at this time, unlike the situation in Scotland and Vienna, their artists and designers were little known by name, the Liberty Style would have been frequently encountered in the pages of *The Studio* magazine, each issue of which was eagerly awaited in Vienna after its first appearance in 1893.

Armchair in white-painted beech designed by Josef Hoffmann c 1903. Height $35\frac{1}{2}$ in.

Fabric design of tulips, poppies and leaves by Harry Napper, Silver Studio, *c*1900, a design which clearly reflects the influence of Archibald Knox who also worked for the Silver Studio.

Design for a wallpaper by C.F.A. Voysey *c*1898. Blue, green and red washes on paper. This design was produced under the title 'Union of Hearts', first as a wallpaper by Essex & Co, then as a textile by Alexander Morton & Co and later as a carpet by Tomkinson & Adams. In all these forms it would have been likely to have been sold by Liberty & Co.

Any definition of the style itself, whatever aspect of design we choose to discuss, must, at its best, embody the idea of the new simplicity of form which in terms of metalwork especially would lead easily and logically to the full acceptance of the machine. Adrian Tilbrook, whose book *The Designs of Archibald Knox for Liberty & Co* is an invaluable contribution to Liberty history, expressed to me his view that Knox was one of the few designers of his period capable of anticipating this trend, intuitively at least: 'I see him as the spiritual father of modern applied design.' Tilbrook also agreed with the view expressed earlier that the shapes and forms which Knox invented are essentially of the twentieth century. In many instances they are the shapes of the space age, with their orbiting loops and arcs (below), spinning hemispheres – floating, seemingly weightless – and rising rocket-like forms (opposite).

The essence of the Liberty Style is the relationship of geometric elements. This assessment also defines the nature of Anglo-Saxon Purism which acted as a scouring agent, banishing the excessive forms of Continental Art Nouveau, and perhaps this Purism in turn had its origin, at least partly, in the fact that so many key contemporary designers, both in England and on the Continent, were architects by training, among them Mackintosh, Voysey and Hoffmann. There is in all the most progressive designs of the period a powerful indication of the clean, sharp lines of architecture extending into all the arenas of applied design. But how, finally, does one define or distinguish the Liberty Style? Primarily, I would suggest, by the originality of its designers, and by the elements of purity, simplicity and clarity of vision which link all these artists, irrespective of their personal style or of the area of design in which they worked.

A highly inventive and revolutionary design by Archibald Knox for a presentation cup and cover set with stones, c 1902. The drawing is inscribed with working notes and in capitals 'Cup'. Height $12\frac{1}{4}$ in. Numbered '3'.

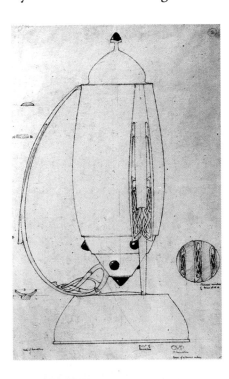

Silver vase set with turquoise matrix, designed by Archibald Knox. An example of the use of space within the object as an element of enrichment: consider the wide curve of the handles and the spaces they create. The decoration is minimal, the plain shapes and forms pure and clean. Height 12 in. Marked L & Co. Cymric. Birmingham date letter for 1902.

The Haseler Connection

CRUCIAL TO THE EVOLUTION of the Liberty Style in the areas of silver, jewellery and pewter manufacture was the firm's association with W. H. Haseler, the Birmingham Manufacturing Goldsmiths and Jewellers. Before this connection began, Liberty silver carried London hallmarks, which continued to be used until 1900–1, overlapping with Liberty's earliest Birmingham mark, which was first registered at the Birmingham Assay Office on 26 September 1899 in the names of J. W. Howe, W. Street and W. H. Haseler. Howe and Street were Arthur Liberty's partners; the third signatory, described as 'Managing Director', was the head of the firm of W. H. Haseler. The merging of the two companies in this venture was to prove richly fruitful, especially to Liberty & Co. They were on the threshold of their greatest creative period.

The partnership with Haseler was further consolidated on 17 May 1901 with the creation of a new company, Liberty & Co (Cymric) Ltd. The original directors of this new company were J. W. Howe and John Llewellyn of Liberty and W. H. and Frank Haseler of the Birmingham firm. But, as Shirley Bury notes in the Liberty centenary exhibition catalogue: 'It was not until nearly two years later [in 1903] that a mark was registered at Birmingham in the name of the new company and even then it was little used. Most articles continued to bear the old Ly & Co mark entered in 1899.' Llewellyn, a gifted young Welshman, had joined Liberty's Silk Department in 1889. His appointment was a momentous one, and he at once began to exert a powerful and fruitful influence on the company. In 1898 he joined the board. Maxwell Haseler, the son of W. H. Haseler, considered Llewellyn to have been a man of great vision crucial to the evolution of the Liberty Style. It is likely that 'Tudric' and 'Cymric' – trade names under which much of Liberty's first metalwork was produced – owe their origin to Llewellyn's Welsh ancestry. Neither is in fact authentic: both were invented names that sounded suitably Celtic.

At precisely the moment that Liberty needed to find a manufacturer able to produce their avant-garde designs, using mass production techniques, they entered into a connection with a firm who were fully equipped to translate their designs into a modern, economic proposition. W. H. Haseler were to make not only the bulk of Liberty Cymric ware, but a little later the whole range of their pewter launched under the title of Tudric. Tudric pewter first appeared in the Liberty catalogues in 1902, but a few designs were available as early as November 1901.

Haseler had all the necessary plant and tools for the manufacture of Liberty silver and pewter products. Although at first Liberty farmed out their orders locally to firms in Soho, they came increasingly to rely on the services of Haseler. On the other hand, the production of metalwork for Liberty was only a small part of Haseler's total turnover. They remained consistently independent goldsmiths and jewellers.

W. R. Haseler O.B.E. (seated) c1914.
William Rabobe Haseler took over the firm of Birmingham jewellers from his father W. H. Haseler in 1896.

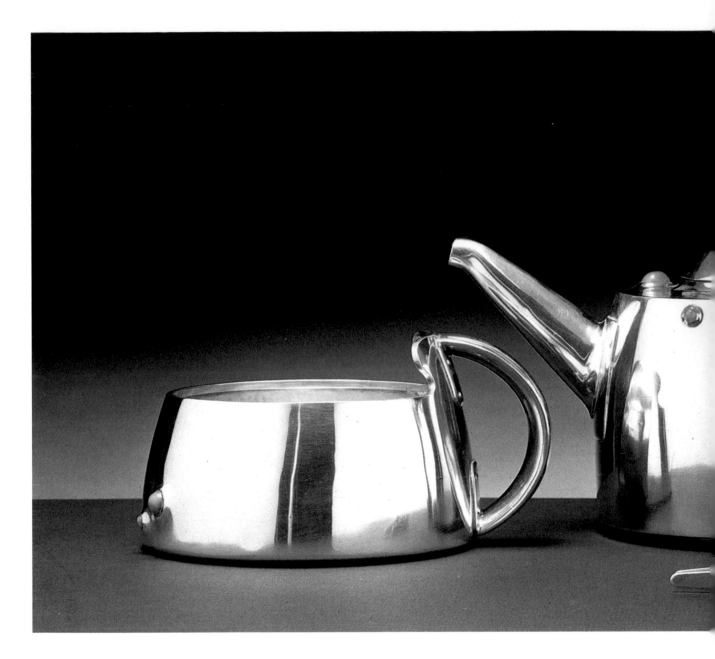

Silver tea-set with cabochon chalcedony
decoration designed by Archibald Knox
c1903 and executed by Liberty & Co. Hallmarked L & Co, Cymric, Bowl $2\frac{3}{4}$ in
high; pot 6 in high; jug $8\frac{1}{4}$ in high; tongs
6 in long.

Spoon described in
Liberty Catalogue No. 62
(1899–1900) as 'fruit or
table spoon'. Designed by
Oliver Baker *c* 1900.
Length 8 in. Maker's
mark: L & Co. Stamped:
Cymric. Bears
Birmingham date letter for
1902.

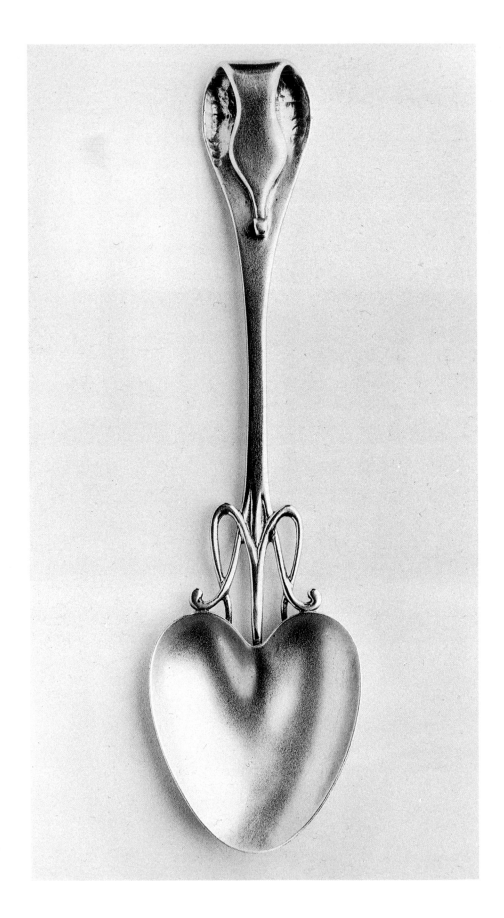

Silver clock with raised foliate design, possibly designed by Archibald Knox. The face is glazed and the numerals enamelled in green and blue, with silver hands terminating in red enamelled hearts. Height 10¼ in. Maker's mark: L & Co. Stamped: Cymric. Bears the Birmingham date letter for 1903.

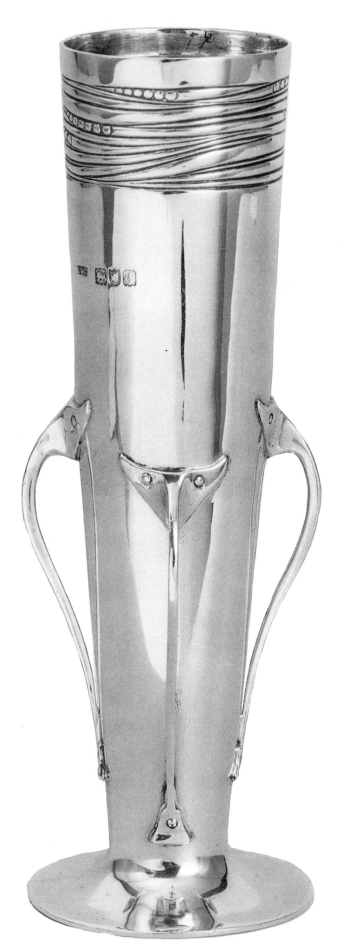

Silver flower vase known as the 'Cyrus'. Silver Studio, London, 1899. Tapering cylinder with a chased frieze near the rim and four riveted handles. The design heralds the emergence of the geometric style. Height $8\frac{1}{2}$ in. Maker's mark: Ly & Co.

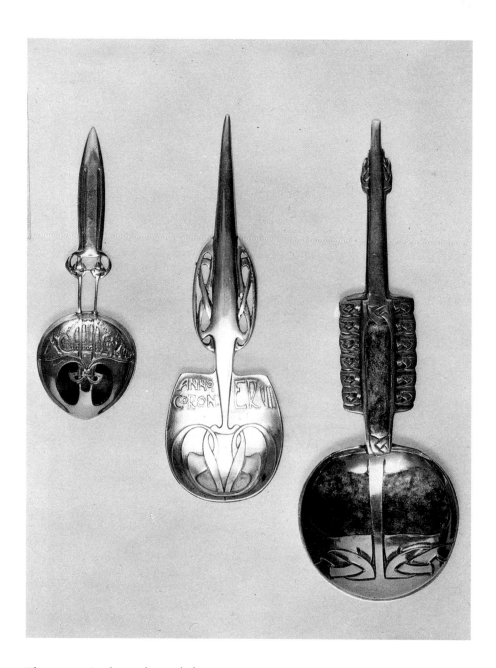

Three spoons in silver and enamel, the middle one an Edward VII Coronation Spoon. All are based on Celtic designs and probably designed by Archibald Knox. Marks: all stamped 'Cymric'. The left and middle ones: 'L & Co' Birmingham date letter for 1901. That on the right bears the Birmingham date letter for 1902. Respective rd nos: 391475/391477/391478. Lengths: $4\frac{7}{8}$ in; $6\frac{1}{2}$ in; $7\frac{3}{4}$ in.

The commercial aspect of the Cymric scheme is suggested by Shirley Bury in the centenary exhibition catalogue. She writes:

> The Cymric scheme was always envisaged as a mass production exercise, even while it incorporated the most recognisable features of Arts and Crafts work, notably the use of semi-precious stones and enamel, and surfaces covered with hammer marks. There was however a difference. The hammer marks left unpolished on the silver made by Ashbee's Guild of Handicrafts and by other workshops associated with the Arts and Crafts Movement were there as the outward and visible signs that each article was made by hand in traditional fashion. Arts and Crafts silver was therefore costly: Cymric wares, while certainly not cheap, were relatively less expensive. Most of the hollow-wares were either spun or were die-stamped flat, complete with the ornament, and then shaped. The cylindrical form of many coffee and tea pots, jugs and other items testifies to this method of construction; an inspection of their interiors shows them to be seamed under the handles. The 'hammer marks' were either cut into the surface of the die, or were genuine, the hammer being used to clean up the surface of the article after stamping.

In this sense hammering was not a 'craft' element but an extension of the finish of a machine-produced object.

This happy marriage of the new aesthetics and the technology of modern machine production was a means of producing the aesthetic artefact in its most economic form.

Shortly before his death I visited Maxwell Haseler at his home in Warwickshire, and he answered many of the questions I raised about the production of Liberty silver and pewter, both then and in a series of letters he wrote to me between January and August 1979. He was an active member of the Haseler company for a great many years and an impeccable authority on its activities. After the formation of the Cymric company in

Above left Silver buckle set with amethysts, coronation spoon and vesta matchbox. The latter, with central decoration in green and blue enamel, was probably designed by Archibald Knox. It is marked L & Co. Cymric, and bears the Birmingham date letter for 1904. The buckle and spoon, marked L & Co 'Cymric', bear Birmingham date letter for 1902.

Left Silver casket with wooden carcass, set with opal matrix. The design, probably by Archibald Knox, is in Celtic style with freely flowing interlacing, the conception strongly but delicately geometric. Length 8½ in. Maker's mark: L & Co. Bears Birmingham date letter for 1903.

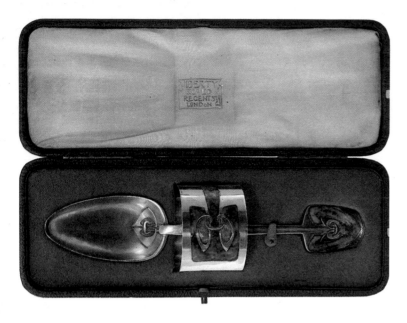

Silver and enamel spoon and napkin ring designed by Archibald Knox, both
chased and ornamented with rich peacock, green and orange enamels.
Marks: L & Co, Cymric. Bears Birmingham date letter for 1902–3.
The silk lining of the original case is gilt stamped with Liberty's mark.

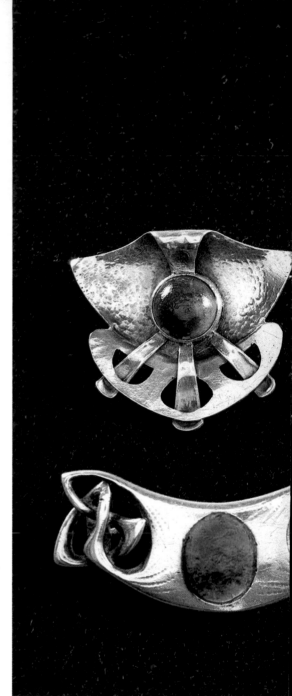

Set of six silver buttons, with enamelled
abstract design, in original box. Each button
is stamped L & Co, Cymric. Birmingham
date letter for 1901.

Top row from left:

Silver and lapis lazuli brooch designed by
  Oliver Baker. Marked Cymric. Width
  $1\frac{1}{8}$ in.
Silver and enamel pendant designed by
  Archibald Knox. Depth $1\frac{3}{4}$ in. Made by
  W. H. Haseler and marked W.H.H.
Silver and enamel brooch designed by
  Archibald Knox. Width $1\frac{1}{8}$ in. Marked
  Murlle Bennett & Co. This company
  frequently supplied small items of
  jewellery to Liberty & Co.

Bottom row from left:

Silver and enamel brooch designed by
  Archibald Knox. Width $1\frac{5}{8}$ in. Marked
  W.H.H.
Silver and enamel brooch, possibly
  designed by Oliver Baker. Width 1 in.
  Marked Liberty & Co.
Silver and enamel pendant designed by
  Archibald Knox. Depth $1\frac{3}{4}$ in. Marked
  L & Co.

All these pieces were either made for
Liberty & Co or sold by them. The dates
are all c 1902–5 and all the designs display
strong geometric qualities.

1901, Liberty acquired the lease of Haseler's Hylton Street premises in Birmingham, together with their plant and tools. However, Haseler continued to make silver stamped with their own mark, and to produce their own catalogues. This was necessary since, as Max Haseler pointed out in one of his letters:

> The trade with Liberty was only a small proportion of our total turnover. I think it was originally treated as an exciting and *potentially* profitable side-line. Liberty was too unconventional for our more conventional customers widely spread throughout the British Isles, and I doubt whether our travellers even carried samples. They would have been far more interested in the goods they *knew* were saleable.

This says a great deal about the advanced nature of Liberty design at this time. The relationship between Liberty and Haseler was perfect. The genius of creation was with Liberty while Haseler provided the machinery and brilliant craftsmanship. Thus idea was matched by form, and by the materials — silver and pewter — that most explicitly gave expression to the Liberty Style.

Max Haseler writes in the same letter:

> Throughout the forty year association of Liberty and Haseler, the production of silver and pewter was left entirely to W.H.Haseler Ltd. Liberty's never interfered in any way and were not interested in any market other than their own shop in Regent Street. The early jewellery and silverware was hand-made (prototypes or 'one-offs' in modern parlance). The jewellery continued to be hand-made, but obviously the silver objects would have been too expensive to continue making entirely by hand — as the market grew — and machinery began to be used in its production, the only condition being that it should not alter the design in any way. At the time — some eighty years

ago – the only machinery in our factories were spinning lathes, small hand-operated presses, and foot-operated drop-stamps. Each design would be carefully studied to devise the cheapest way to produce it. Cylindrical articles would be spun and the decoration chased, embossed, or incised by hand. Small articles like waist clasps, buckles, tea and coffee spoons, caddy spoons and buttons would be die-stamped. Any perforation in the design would be pierced by hand-saw.

As regards the pewter, almost all the designs of Knox had a raised decoration which was too expensive to hand chase, so that casting from moulds was the only solution. The outlay on moulds was high and the process slow, but of course the number of pewter articles made far out-numbered the silver. I think it would be true to say that all the early pieces of pewter were cast. A pewter article which has been cast is far superior in every way to one that has been spun.

Max Haseler also described for me in detail some aspects of the technical methods used by his firm to perfect the forms that Arthur Liberty and his designers required. Perfection of technique in working the metals was an integral part of the realization of Liberty design ideas. It is greatly to the credit of John Llewellyn, who first saw samples of Haseler's jewellery in a London hotel, that the bond between the two firms was established. Llewellyn recognized instantly that here were the craftsmen for the manufacture of Cymric silver and, later, of all Liberty's pewterware. Max Haseler began by describing the difference between German pewter and that produced by his firm for Liberty. He pointed out that Kayser ware – or Kayserzinn as it is now marked and best known (p. 108) – contained a high proportion of lead which produced a coarse, dark discoloration of the metal. Form and design apart, one can easily distinguish the discoloration of unpolished Kayserzinn as being essentially different from that of unpolished Liberty pewter. All pewter – English and

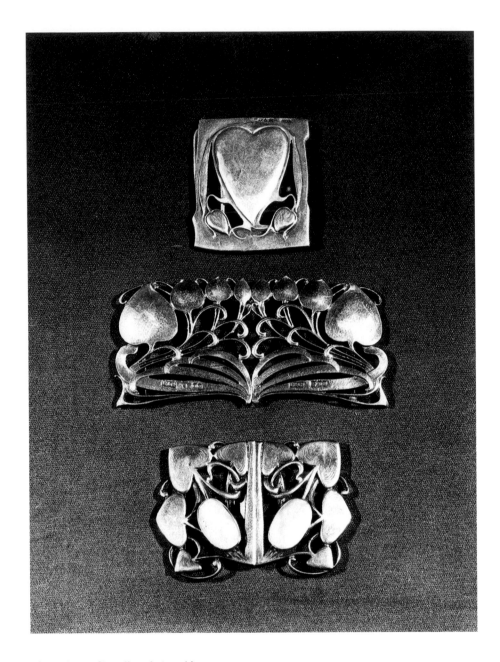

Three pieces of jewellery designed by
Archibald Knox: *top* Silver buckle,
London 1900. Height 2⅜ in. Marked: Ly
& Co; *centre* Silver waist clasp, London
1899. Length 4½ in. Marked: Ly & Co;
bottom Silver waist clasp set with blister
pearls. Length 3 in. Birmingham date letter
for 1902. Marked: Ly & Co.

Gold necklace with turquoise matrix setting
and baroque pearls, designed by Archibald
Knox *c* 1900. Length of chain 16 in. No
marks.

Continental — was originally meant to shine and resemble silver. It is usually found today in antique and junk shops in its dull, discoloured form, though it can be re-polished. Liberty pewter is never as dark, as 'black', as Kayserzinn. The fact that Liberty pewter does not discolour so much is simply because the original composition of the metal used by Haseler contained no lead. It was composed as follows: 90 per cent tin, 8 per cent copper and 2 per cent antimony. It is a common mistake to think that it contained some silver; it did not.

Max Haseler went on to detail the firm's method of casting. All pewter was made from iron moulds. These were suspended on pulleys over large vats of water, the pewter composition was poured in, and the mould lowered to a little above the surface of the water. It was not dipped immediately but splashed with water by a second caster. The mould and its contents were thus cooled gradually before complete immersion took place. The result of this method, perfected by Haseler's craftsmen, was to produce a fine cast completely free of disfiguring bubbles. Although in many ways the Cymric and Tudric products bore a superficial resemblance to the products of the Arts and Crafts Movement, so far as Haseler's work for Liberty was concerned, once the design had been drawn there was little further contact between the designer and the manufacturer. The end product was no longer 'handicraft' but a machine-made object.

Despite the modified 'craft' appearance of many of the finished articles,

Pewter tea service and tray designed by Hugo Leven and made by J.P. Kayser & Sons, Krefeld (Kayserzinn) *c* 1896–7. Length of tray 21½ in. Hugo Leven was one of the most distinguished German designers of the period, and his tea-set makes an interesting comparison with that designed by Archibald Knox *c* 1903 (pp. 94–5). Both sets reveal the elements of the geometric-abstract revolution which was then taking place in the field of the applied arts.

they were meant to be produced – as they were later – in large quantities using such machine processes as Max Haseler described to me. The main concession to the hand was a degree of hammering which simulated the 'hand-made' look of the article, and was to some extent admissible in the manufacture of such small items as jewellery and clasps. But the process was – and rightly – generally frowned upon both by the designer and the manufacturer, who were conscious of the advance of technology and the inconsistency which lay in trying to mask the clean, sharp character of machine-produced articles with the suggestion of handicraft. It was only after the main impetus of the Liberty revolution had lost its creative momentum that hammering became fashionable for many of the pieces of pewter produced in the 1920s. But these pieces, often modified or extensively altered versions of early designs, and carrying late numbers, are outside the scope and character of the Liberty Style proper.

The zenith of Liberty's creative pewter production had been reached well before the outbreak of the First World War (Arthur Liberty died in 1917). As early as 1909–10 Liberty had begun to sell many of Knox's designs to Connell & Co of Cheapside who produced their own, inferior versions of Liberty ware.

Pewter desk set designed by Archibald Knox *c*1902–3, comprising an inkwell (height 3½ in), stamp box with blue-green enamel decoration on lid, pen nib box, adjustable photograph frame on easel stand and pen tray. Various marks: Tudric, English Pewter, Made by Liberty & Co. Nos range from 099 to 0141.

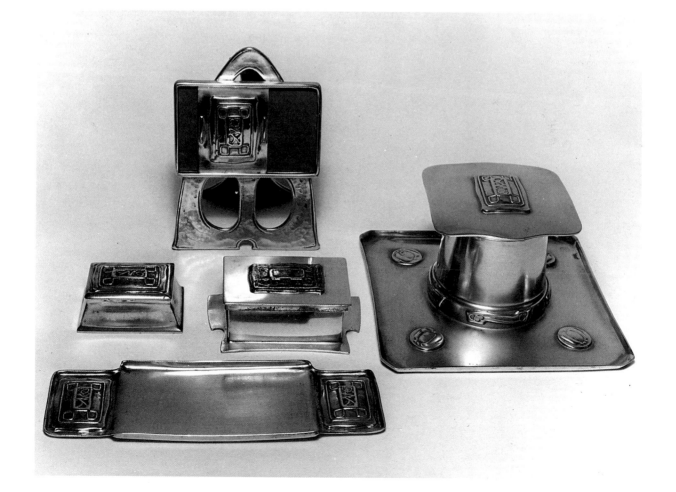

Right Pewter vase,
c 1903–4, in which space is
used as an integral part of
the design. Height 9¾ in.
Marked : Tudric 029.

Far right Pewter decanter
c 1903 by Archibald
Knox, the green glass by
James Powell & Sons of
Whitefriars. Height 11⅞ in.
Mark : Tudric 0308.

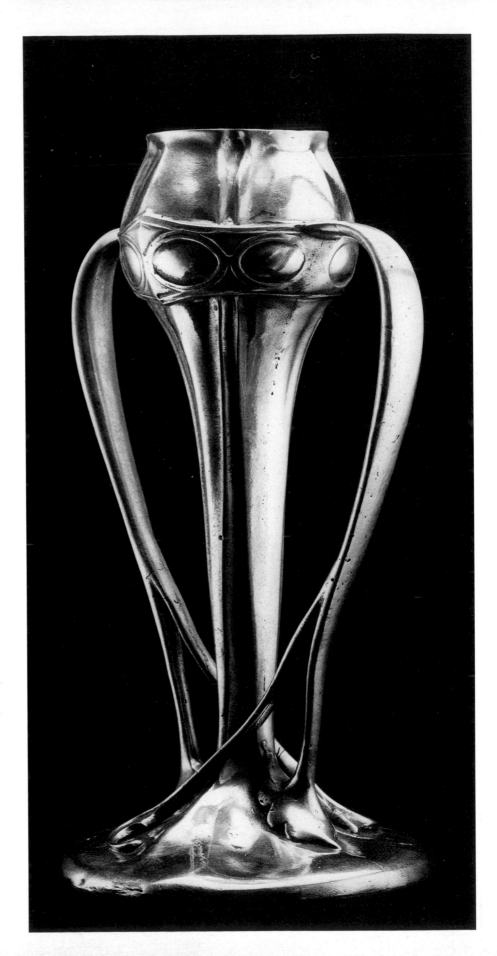

Pewter candlestick, probably designed by
Archibald Knox *c* 1903. The inversion of
forms and proportions – such as the cone
shape – is one of the more revolutionary
features of the Liberty Style. The discreet
Celtic decoration is a perfect foil for the
naked simplicity of the overall form.
Marked Tudric 0221.

Pewter candlestick, *c* 1903. Height 8⅞ in. Marked:
English Pewter, 0223.

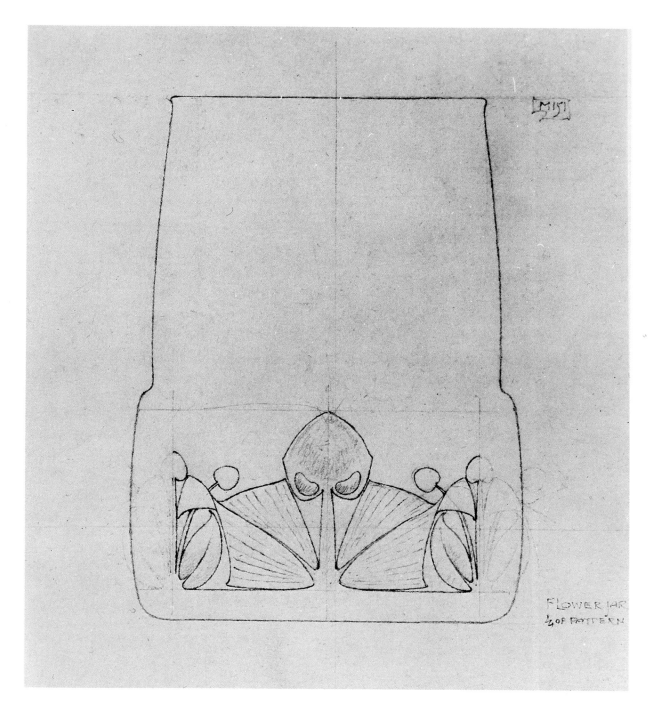

Design for a flower jar by Archibald Knox,
c 1902–3. Inscribed with working notes,
this, like other working drawings, affords
an invaluable glimpse of the way in which
the artist thought out his designs. The
drawings, virtually those of an architectural
draughtsman, are always clean and sharp
and would seem to confirm the years
(1892–6) when Knox is believed to have
worked part-time with the architect-
designer M. H. Baillie Scott on the Isle of
Man.

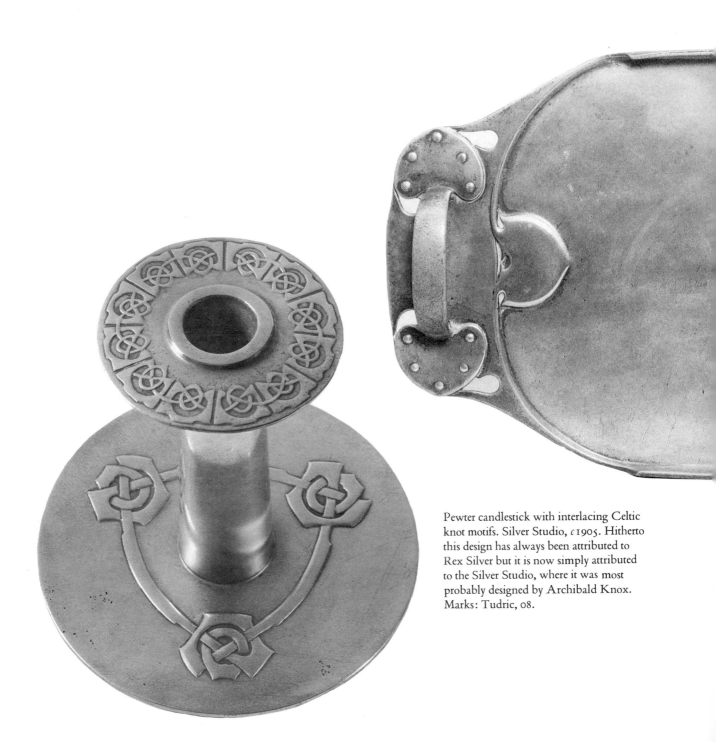

Pewter candlestick with interlacing Celtic knot motifs. Silver Studio, *c* 1905. Hitherto this design has always been attributed to Rex Silver but it is now simply attributed to the Silver Studio, where it was most probably designed by Archibald Knox. Marks: Tudric, 08.

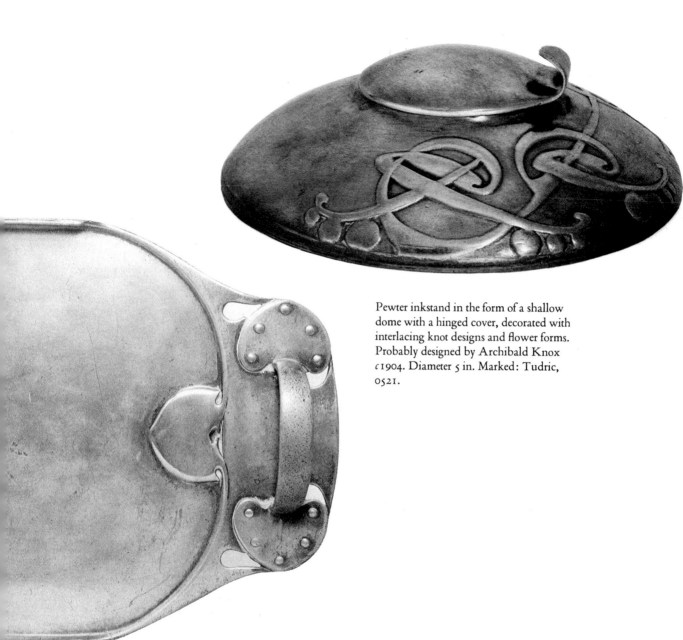

Pewter inkstand in the form of a shallow
dome with a hinged cover, decorated with
interlacing knot designs and flower forms.
Probably designed by Archibald Knox
*c*1904. Diameter 5 in. Marked: Tudric,
0521.

Pewter tray decorated with heart-shaped
motifs, *c*1901. The use of rivets, of which
Knox was particularly fond, suggests that it
was one of his designs. Marked: Tudric,
042.

Left Pewter clock by Archibald Knox
c 1901, with numerals of an imaginative
design, enamelled hands and abalone insets.
Mark: Tudric.

Right Pewter clock *c* 1903, probably
designed by Archibald Knox and perhaps
best described as Liberty Style Futurism.
Height 7½ in. Marks: Tudric, 0245.

Two green glass decanters mounted in pewter, *c* 1903.
The smaller one is marked Tudric, Rd nos. 426580
and 0310; the larger is described on page 110. The
conception of both these designs typifies the
revolutionary approach of the Liberty Style to the
problem of rethinking the organization of traditional
forms.

Right Chocolate drinking mug in pewter. The handle would originally have been caned. The acute geometric stylization of the plant motifs contrasts sharply with the traditional shape of the mug. Nevertheless, this is an instance where the traditional and the avant-garde are perfectly complementary. Height $5\frac{1}{2}$ in. Marks: English Pewter, Made by Liberty & Co and Solkets mark.

Cylindrical pewter biscuit box, flared at the base and decorated with small stylized heart-shaped flowers, *c*1902–3. Height 7 in. Marked: Tudric 059.

Marks and Numbers

THE IDENTIFICATION of Liberty products by marks and labels is simple with furniture and mirrors, a little more difficult with silver, and very complicated when it comes to the marking of pewter, which can take many forms.

Where ivorine labels are attached to the backs of mirrors, or to furniture, they are usually oblong, about two inches by half an inch and carry the words 'Liberty, London' or 'Liberty, London and Paris', occasionally, 'Liberty, Birmingham'. Sometimes the earlier pieces of furniture carry small oval labels, convex and enamelled in white. But these are relatively rare. Labels were originally attached by small nails, but are often missing for one reason or another. So the absence of a label does not mean that the piece in question is *not* by Liberty. One can identify items by style. Or a piece may at least be 'in the Liberty style', a term one often finds in sale room catalogues where positive identification is impossible. One must always bear in mind that designers as distinguished as C.F.A. Voysey often worked anonymously for Liberty. This applies in particular to Voysey textile and wallpaper designs. One can, of course, look for and frequently find on a piece of furniture, or the back of a mirror, the oblong (or oval) area of discoloration which indicates that at some time it carried a label.

The identification of silver can be made along the following lines. As with all correctly assayed British silver, Liberty silver carries standard marks: the town mark (e.g. an anchor for Birmingham, a leopard's head for London), the silver mark (the lion *passant*) and the date letter (see opposite). These are preceded by the maker's mark. In the case of Cymric ware, this name also appears somewhere in the proximity of the other marks. For silver the earliest Liberty maker's mark was 'Ly & Co' but this does not appear to have been used after 1900.

The marking and numbering of pewter is far more complex. Let us deal with the marks first. These can range from 'Tudric' with a number, sometimes with 'Made in England', and sometimes with the 'Solkets' mark and the crossed acorn motif. Solkets was one of the Haseler marks, and derives from the fact, as Maxwell Haseler told me, that his father's firm

Reverse side of a Liberty silver buckle
showing system of assay marking. Maker's
mark (L & Co); town mark (an anchor for
Birmingham); sterling mark (lion passant);
date letter ('b' for 1901); and, in this case,
the Cymric mark.

were originally jewellers specializing in the manufacture of solitaires and lockets. To these marks can be added 'English Pewter' and 'Made by Liberty & Co'. These can appear in any combination. I have seen pieces marked only 'Tudric', and pieces with only a number. Usually the word Tudric is enclosed in a sunken rectangle, with the letters standing out in relief. Occasionally the letters are impressed and enclosed in quotes. Now for the question of numbering. Occasionally one will find a piece that only carries a number, in which case it has to be judged stylistically. Registration numbers may also appear. The system began in 1830 to prevent the illegal copying of patented designs. Until 1883 the format was that of a lozenge such as one frequently finds on Victorian pottery and porcelain. After that it became a series of digits preceded by the abbreviation 'Rd' for Registered (p. 124). Numbers themselves presumably distinguished the specific mould, model or design and were provided to help clients in ordering or re-ordering. Or the number may have been given by the Liberty studios and buyer of the day to the artists' original working drawings, of which the Victoria and Albert Museum possesses a substantial quantity.

The main point to bear in mind is that the lower numbers – usually preceded by an '0' – are the earliest pieces, and that with five figure numbers – inclusive of the '0' – we are moving into the 1920s. The best of the early pieces, including most of the designs by Knox, are around the 0500 mark. Many early designs were repeated, often with savage modifications in the 1920s. These, and other typical Twenties designs – usually plain and fully hammered – carry five digits.

One must remember that the height of the pewter period was somewhere around 1905, by which time all the best of the Knox designs had been made. The two-branched candlestick usually attributed to Knox (opposite) carries the number 0530 and dates from 1905. After this there was a gradual decline in the design of Liberty pewter.

But there are no absolute and final rules about either the marking or the numbering of Liberty pewter.

Two-branched candlestick in pewter, probably designed by Archibald Knox. 1905. The straightness of the central column, partly decorated with pierced leaves and berries on tendrils, is offset by the curve of the arm. Parts of the design are left plain, in sharp and effective contrast to the richly decorated areas. Marked: Made in England, Solkets, Rd No. 459548. 0530.

Marks found on Liberty pewter

Registration marks were introduced as early as 1830 to prevent the pirating of an object by a competitor. In 1883 their format was changed from that of a lozenge to a series of digits, the letters 'Rd' being short for Registered.

The trade or brand name for the pewter range.

A variation of the 'Tudric' mark above. This brand name appears frequently, in both forms, and in combination with other marks such as 'Made in England' and, as here, with the 'Solkets' mark.

A rarely used Liberty mark, in this case stamped on one piece of a small three-piece tea set. The type face is identical to that used in the 'Tudric' name stamp.

Presumably the mould or model number intended for reference and ordering. It is also a key to the date of the item. The figures 0375 would place it *c* 1904–5.

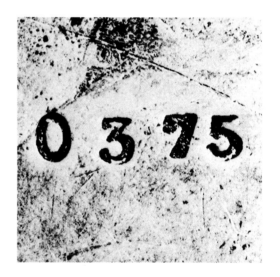

An unusual mark normally occurring on large salvers or platters but not solely restricted to such pieces. Usually reserved for less crudely decorated stems.

The imprint 'Solkets' under crossed acorns was a mark sometimes used by W.H. Haseler & Co on Tudric pewterware.

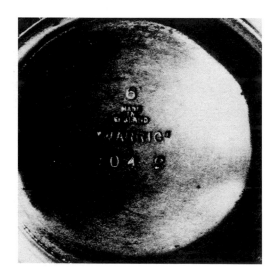

Mark found on pewter bearing decoration identical to that on certain Liberty & Co items. This mark dates from about 1920 and either indicates yet another Liberty brand name or that the design had been sold to a company trading under the name of 'Warric'. The latter would seem more likely.

Tudric mark incorporating that of another firm, in this case 'Glossoid Co'. A combination mark such as this would usually have been used when a large number of objects was commissioned for a specific purpose, e.g. as presentation tankards for all the members of a golf club. In this case, Glossoid, acting as agents, would have commissioned Liberty & Co to produce objects linking their name with the Liberty Tudric mark in order to add prestige to the piece.

Gold printed mark often found on the fabric inside the lid of a
jewellery box or on the lid of a box intended for presentation.

Connell & Co stamp (see p. 136). Such pieces would frequently bear
Liberty & Co mould numbers and other marks, presumably because
the manufacturers had not altered the original moulds when the
design ownership changed hands.

Unusual mark found on pieces manufactured by Liberty & Co in
the 1920s. Many such designs continued to be produced until the
early 1930s.

The placing of silver marks is arbitrary. They can appear in any order or position on the item. Here the 'Cymric' mark appears above the pin and the maker's mark above the standard assay marks: the anchor for Birmingham, the sterling mark (lion passant) and the date letter 'c' for 1902.

Most of the silver produced by Liberty & Co seems to have been assayed in either London or Birmingham, the earliest pieces in London. Here we have the leopard for London and the date letter 'd' for 1899.

Hand engraved registration number. Owing to the skill and time involved in execution, these script numerals were restricted to the larger and more expensive pieces.

The base of a silver tankard showing the scratched numerals and letters employed by the jewellery trade, and also by pawnbrokers, as a reference. Such marks are known as the 'scratch rate', a trade system indicating the weight of the item when it was made. It enabled jewellers to tell at a later weighing whether for any reason the piece had lost some of its original weight.

An example of a Liberty & Co set of silver marks.

A variation of the above, although this mark does not appear to have been used after 1900.

A third variation of the Liberty & Co maker's mark restricted to the year 1903.

As with pewter, silver items were registered at the Public Records Office.

Machine-punched variation of the hand-engraved registration mark.

Directory of Liberty Manufacturers

I HAVE INCLUDED brief references to manufacturers known to have worked in association with Liberty & Co, or to have supplied them with lines from their own stocks for sale in the company's Regent Street shop. Their work does not necessarily meet the terms of reference of the Liberty Style *per se*, but they are listed because many of their products show, often surprisingly, the influence of that style as I have endeavoured to describe and illustrate it.

Other firms are included because their products carry the mark 'Made for Liberty & Co', but the variations in marking are so wide and inconsistent that many pieces clearly made for Liberty do not carry this designation. Lack of records in every area make stylistic identification an adventurous necessity. The list is included primarily to demonstrate just how extensive were the contacts and associations of Liberty & Co with a great many other firms and factories, both in Britain and abroad.

ALLER VALE POTTERY, *Newton Abbot, Devon*

This pottery began making brown ware from 1865 and in 1868 was taken over by John Phillips. In 1887 the works became known as the Aller Vale Art Pottery. Liberty & Co stocked their wares between the years 1887 and 1901. Their work is often adventurous, the decoration free and bold. Impressed mark.

MURLLE BENNET & CO, *London*

This firm frequently supplied small items of Art Nouveau style jewellery to Liberty & Co during the early years of the present century. They specialized in pendants and brooches, usually enamelled. Their designs frequently follow the typical Liberty Art Nouveau style of the early years, but are sweeter and prettier than the purer and more geometric designs of Archibald Knox. Murlle Bennett & Co were an Anglo-German firm who frequently advertised as their own productions pieces which appeared in the Liberty and W.H.Haseler catalogues. This was not uncommon practice at a time when there was a great deal of pilfering and pirating of the designs of other firms. These were often just sufficiently modified as to appear 'original'. A lot of the Murlle Bennett jewellery sold through Liberty & Co was probably made in Pforzheim, although the pieces often carried the marks of both Liberty and Haseler. There has always been some confusion about the exact nature of this firm's activities. Their jewellery was close to the Liberty and Arts and Crafts styles, but was also influenced by the contemporary German geometric style. Their claim to have designed all their jewellery is belied by their advertisements, which illustrate pieces supposedly exclusive to Liberty and which appear in the catalogues of that firm. They also supplied Connell of Cheapside and the Goldsmiths' Company with jewellery.

C.H.BRANNAM LTD, *Barnstaple, Devon*

Brannam's operated from Litchdon Street Pottery in Barnstaple, and were notable for their grotesque and fantastic motifs: animals, birds, sea creatures and dragons. They frequently used the old Roman name 'Barum' for Barnstaple as their trade mark, but their marks are extremely varied, from incised markings in a cursive script to impressed markings in capital letters, often including the words 'Made for Liberty'. Early pieces are usually signed in a cursive script with the date, and often the initials of the designer such as 'J.D.' (John Dewdney) or 'W.B.' (William Baron).

In 1882 Liberty & Co became the sole agents for C.H.Brannam and remained so until 1914, when control of the firm passed into the hands of Brannam's two sons. They continued to supply Liberty with pottery until the 1930s.

GIUSEPPE CANTIGALLI, *Florence*

Italian pottery whose wares were sold by Liberty & Co in the late 1880s and 1890s. They made glazed earthenware with painted decoration in bronze lustres and blues.

Pewter owl jug with sea-shell eyes,
*c*1902–3. The prototype of this design was a
pottery owl jug made for Liberty by
C.H.Brannam of Barnstaple in about 1900.
Height 8 in. Marked: Tudric 035.

Vase with yellow glaze by C.H.Brannam,
*c*1905–10. Typical of Brannam's work for
Liberty & Co, it demonstrates the strong
influence of the Celtic style. Impressed
marks: C.H.Brannam. Barum.N. Devon.;
'Made for Liberty & Co' within a
rectangle.

COMPTON POTTERY, *Guildford, Surrey*

Mary Fraser Tytler, wife of the Victorian painter George Frederick Watts, founded the Compton Pottery in 1902 and produced a range of garden pottery for Liberty & Co, many items from Celtic designs originally created by Archibald Knox. Impressed mark.

Above Garden urn in glazed turquoise manufactured at the Compton Pottery from a design by Archibald Knox. Punchmark on the inside reads: 'Designed and Manufactured for Liberty & Co'.

Right Liberty advertisement for garden ornaments made by the Compton Pottery. (From *The Book of Garden Ornaments*, 1904.)

GARDEN POTS AND SUNDIALS

FLOWER POT.   THE " REGIN " DESIGN.
Frost Proof.

Height	Width	Price
1 ft. 6 in.	1 ft. 9 in.	£3 3 0

Regd. Design.

MESSRS CONNELL & CO OF CHEAPSIDE, *London*

Liberty sold off many exhausted lines of pewter to this firm who produced their own adapted versions, often from original designs by Archibald Knox. Adrian Tilbrook notes in *The Designs of Archibald Knox for Liberty & Co* (p. 49) that Connell 'attempted somewhat unsuccessfully to compete with the Tudric range of pewter. Their shapes, however, were always traditional and the use of blue and green ceramic tablets was seldom as effective as the electric blue and marine green so often employed by Liberty & Co.' Most of the Knox designs were sold to Messrs Connell around 1909–10 when the demand for this style of pewter was beginning to wane.

JAMES COUPER & SONS, *Glasgow*

Makers of Clutha glass, mainly designed by Christopher Dresser and sometimes by George Watton, and extensively used by Liberty & Co as liners for their pewter ware, particularly for designs by Archibald Knox (see p. 30).

DELLA ROBBIA POTTERY, *Birkenhead, Cheshire*

This factory was started in 1894 by Harold Rathbone and Conrad Dressler and closed again only seven years later, in 1901. The firm specialized in tiles, earthenware and particularly relief plaques inspired by the panels, reliefs and fountains created in Florence by the sculptor Luca della Robbia and his family. Mark: 'della Robbia', incised or impressed with ship device and often the initials of designers and decorators. For instance: 'C' for Charles Collis, 'C.A.W.' for C.A. Walker, 'C.M.' for Carlo Manzoni, 'L.W.' for Liza Wilkins and 'R.B.' for Ruth Bare. Their work was widely sold by Liberty & Co between the years 1894 and 1901.

FARNHAM POTTERIES, *Farnham, Surrey*

Managed by A. Harris & Son and operating as early as 1893, Farnham Pottery was sold in large quantities by Liberty's. Their ceramics appear in the Liberty catalogues of the day as 'Green Ware'. The shapes are often simple and similar to those of the Brannam ware produced around 1915–16. Marks: see Godden's encyclopaedia (Bibliography).

GOUDA, *Arnhem*

This Dutch pottery centre produced highly colourful and distinctive pottery frequently bearing the mark 'Made for Liberty'.

Gouda vase made in Holland c 1910. Height $2\frac{3}{4}$ in. Marked Liberty & Co.

W. H. HASELER & CO, *Birmingham*

Goldsmiths, silversmiths and jewellers, founded in 1870 by William Hair Haseler. The firm of Haseler & Co went into formal partnership with Liberty & Co in 1901 when the two firms joined forces to launch the Cymric silver scheme under the title of Liberty & Co (Cymric) Ltd.

J. P. KAYSER & SONS, *Krefeld, Germany*

German metalwork firm founded in 1885 near Düsseldorf by Jean Kayser. From the mid-1890s they manufactured pewter Jugendstil objects such as ashtrays, lamps, beakers, vases, tea and coffee sets best known as 'Kayserzinn'. Their main designer was Hugo Leven, a name to be compared with that of Liberty's main pewter designer, Archibald Knox.

L. LICHTINGER, *Munich*

German pewter manufacturers from whom Arthur Liberty imported pewter, mainly tableware, for sale in his Regent Street shop from 1899.

E. LITTLER & CO, *Merton Abbey, Surrey*

Block printed textiles and scarves were printed for Liberty by Littler & Co. (William Morris also had his print works at Merton Abbey but his property was downstream from Littler's works. 'We sent our dirty water down to Morris!' was a favourite Liberty remark.) In 1904 Liberty took over the works, and they acquired the freehold in 1922. By the 1890s Liberty were taking up the whole of Littler's production. The firm continued to hand print there until 1973 when the premises were sold.

LOETZ (OR LÖTZ) WITWE, *Klostermühle, Austria*

Founded in 1836, Loetz were glass manufacturers, particularly celebrated for their fine iridescent glass, comparable in type with Tiffany. It was sold by Liberty & Co in the 1890s. Marks: two crossed arrows with star in each intersection, with 'Loetz, Austria'; crossed arrows in circle with 'Lötz'; crossed arrows in circle with 'Lötz, Klostermühle'.

JOHN MONCRIEFF LTD, *Perth, Scotland*

Scottish glass makers founded by John Moncrieff, *c*1864. They produced heavy glassware, mainly Art Deco, streaked with various colours and inclusions within the body of the glass, which was sold by Liberty & Co in the 1920s and 1930s, but earlier examples are coming to light. Monart glass, as it was known, was unmarked except for a paper label affixed to the base. Pieces still carrying the original label are naturally rare.

WILLIAM MOORCROFT, *Staffordshire*

David Coachworth wrote in the Liberty centenary exhibition catalogue, 'Arguably the most important and lasting connection formed by Liberty's with a producer of ceramics was that with the well known artist-potter William Moorcroft. A.L.Liberty first encountered Moorcroft in 1898, when the latter was in sole charge of the art pottery workshop of the firm of James Macintyre & Co at Burslem. The two men rapidly became friends, and Liberty's began to sell Moorcroft's earliest range of "Florian" ware.' After 1913, when Moorcroft left James Macintyre & Co to start his own workshops at Cobridge, he continued to supply Liberty & Co with such lines as 'Hazledene' (trees in landscape setting), 'Claremont' (toadstools) and the green and red 'Flaminian' ware which he created specially for Liberty. Some pieces of Moorcroft, such as vases and tazzas, were set in Tudric pewter bases. Many pieces carry the mark 'Made for Liberty' (see Moorcroft in list of exhibition catalogues). Signature W.Moorcroft in bold script always appears. Until the 1920s this is invariably in green, after which it is mainly blue.

'Hazledene' vase designed by William Moorcroft and produced by James Macintyre & Co, *c*1902. The stylized design of trees suggests great height and space. Height 9$\frac{3}{8}$ in. Signed by the artist. Printed mark: Made for Liberty & Co, Rd No. 397964.

Two examples of William Moorcroft's 'Claremont' (toadstools) design specially made for Liberty. The stylization of the toadstools and the general form of the design is relatively revolutionary for 1903. In a 'Bric-a-Brac' Liberty catalogue (No. 101, page 28, *c* 1905) it is stated that, 'The motif and the name were suggested by a peculiar kind of fungi growing in the woods on the estate of the Duchess of Albany.' Large vase height $7\frac{1}{8}$ in, small vase height $4\frac{1}{4}$ in. Signed 'W. Moorcroft' and marked 'Made for Liberty'. Rd No. 420081. The number indicates that the design was registered in 1903.

Right Large gourd-shaped vase by William Moorcroft: red 'Flaminian' design, 1905. Set with circular motifs based on a swirl of abstracted flower forms. Signed by the poster. Marked: Made for Liberty, Rd No. 452777.

ALEXANDER MORTON & CO, *Kilmarnock, Scotland*

Morton's power loom carpet and textile factory produced carpets and tapestries designed by William Morris (not for Liberty) and C.F.A. Voysey. The man responsible for the association between Liberty & Co and both Littler's (*c.f.*) hand printing works and Alexander Morton's factory was the imaginative and enterprising young Welshman John Llewellyn. Morton's became weavers for Liberty in the 1890s, manufacturing all styles of Liberty design in woven fabrics.

'OSIRIS' (See WALTER SCHERF & CO)

'ORIVIT', *Cologne, Germany*

General pewter manufacturers whose products Liberty sold in the early 1900s. Mark: 'ORIVIT'.

PILKINGTON LANCASTRIAN POTTERY, *Clifton Junction, Lancashire*

Established in 1892, Pilkington's were manufacturers of tiles, vases and bowls, some pieces decorated with designs by Walter Crane, the tiles often by Crane and Voysey. They were sold by Liberty & Co in the early 1900s. Marks various: see Godden (Bibliography).

JAMES POWELL & SONS, *Whitefriars, London*

Glassmakers who provided Liberty & Co with distinctive green glass liners for their metalwork.

ROYAL DOULTON, *Staffordshire and London*

Liberty sold a variety of Doulton lines, many decorated with characteristic Art Nouveau designs such as stylized plant motifs. Marks various: see Godden (Bibliography).

WALTER SCHERF & CO, *Nuremberg, Germany*

Manufacturers of pewter produced under the trade name of 'Osiris' and sold by Liberty & Co at the turn of the century. Mark 'Osiris'.

SILVER STUDIO, *Hammersmith, London*

General design studio established in 1880 by Arthur Silver (1853–96). These studios provided Liberty & Co with textile designs, pewter, silver and jewellery, and many designs for Cymric ware. Later, Arthur's eldest son Reginald 'Rex' Silver directed the practice, at first with his brother Harry and then by himself. After Arthur Silver's early death, it was directed by Harry Napper (*q.v.*) until Rex came of age. It continued until 1963.

WILLIAM HOWSON TAYLOR, *West Smethwick, Birmingham*

English art potter who established the Ruskin Pottery in 1898, producing Ruskin pottery 'buttons' which were often set into Liberty mirror surrounds or into the lids of boxes. Colours, rich and high-fired, ranged from dark blues and greens to turquoise, apple green, purple and mauve. For marks see Godden (Bibliography)

THOMAS WARDLE, *Leek*

Fabric printers to Liberty & Co in the 1880s, specializing in oriental silks.

Directory of Artists and Designers

As in the case of the firms and manufacturers known to have supplied Liberty & Co with stock — some of it expressly designed for them — many of the designers and artists whose names are included in the following list were not necessarily directly connected with the concept of the Liberty Style. However, a working knowledge of the artists and designers associated with the firm is both interesting and helpful in creating a clear picture of Liberty's wide associations. (Artists' dates are given where known.)

M. H. Baillie-Scott (1865–1945)

English architect, furniture and textile designer, Baillie-Scott also worked with metal and ceramics, producing designs for Liberty & Co from 1893.

Oliver Baker (1856–1939)

A Birmingham painter and designer, and a frequent exhibitor at the Royal Academy from 1883, Oliver Baker was a key figure in the Liberty Cymric scheme for which he produced many designs. He also designed pewter for the firm.

William Birch

William Birch, a furniture maker of High Wycombe, provided Liberty & Co with chairs and some cabinet furniture at the turn of the century. In 1901 he was joined by E. G. Punnett (*qv*).

Charles Hubert Brannam (1855–1937)

(See C. H. Brannam Ltd)

Lindsay P. Butterfield (1896–1948)

A fabric designer who worked for Liberty & Co in the 1890s. His work was based mainly on stylized floral motifs.

WALTER CRANE (1845–1915)

A designer and illustrator, Walter Crane was closely associated with William Morris and the Arts and Crafts Movement. He designed fabrics for Liberty & Co in the 1890s.

H. C. CRAYTHORN (1881–1949)

Craythorn was a silversmith and designer and a pupil of Arthur Gaskin. His brilliant talents were recognized by W.H.Haseler in 1898 when Craythorn was seventeen. He worked for Haseler's for some forty years and produced most of the designs executed by them for Liberty & Co. His most distinguished and now celebrated work, designed by Archibald Knox and executed by Craythorn, is the silver casket supplied by Liberty to the Rockefeller family c1900 and now in the Museum of Modern Art, New York.

BERNARD CUZNER (1877–1956)

A silversmith and jeweller who designed many items for Liberty & Co around 1900–5.

DR CHRISTOPHER DRESSER (1834–1904)

Botanist, designer, metalworker and writer on art and the principles of art and design, Dresser, born in Glasgow, was a key figure in the history of modern design. In contrast to his early enthusiasm for the Japanese taste and the Aesthetic Movement, he was a radical and revolutionary designer of glass and metalwork who fully accepted the machine and the approach to modern methods of mass production, and demonstrated a remarkable ability to anticipate the Bauhaus manner as early as 1879. He was a close friend of Arthur Lasenby Liberty who owned shares in the Bond Street firm, the Art Furnishers Alliance, of which Dresser became manager in 1880. In 1883 this firm went into liquidation, and in 1889 Dresser moved to Barnes in West London where he ran a studio with the help of some ten assistants. Among them were Archibald Knox and almost certainly Rex Silver of the Silver Studio (*qv*). His son Louis joined the furniture department of Liberty & Co in 1896. Dresser's main practical association with Liberty's was through the design of Clutha glass (see page 33 and James Couper entry, page 136).

ELEANOR FORTESCUE-BRICKDALE (1871–1945)

A designer and enamel painter for Liberty & Co who specialized in figurative painting, such as friezes for bowls, depicting figures in landscape settings. She was also a book illustrator and painter.

ARTHUR and GEORGIE GASKIN (1862–1928 and 1868–1934)

A husband and wife team – painters, illustrators and metalworkers – who designed jewellery for Liberty & Co during the first decade of the century from their Birmingham Studios.

E. W. GODWIN (1833–86)

An English architect and furniture designer, widely known for his Anglo-Japanese style furniture, Godwin was a passionate supporter of the cult of Japonisme. He was appointed supervisor of the Costume Department at Liberty & Co on 17 January 1884 at an agreed fee of 'one guinea for each hour in the studio. The hours in any one week were not to exceed six hours ...' (see Adburgham, Bibliography).

A. E. JONES (1879–1954)

Jones, a Birmingham jeweller, produced a number of designs for Liberty

& Co. Less well known than his contemporary and associate Bernard Cuzner, he was considered very promising in his day.

JESSIE M. KING (1876–1949)

A Scottish painter, designer and book illustrator, Jessie King studied at the Glasgow School of Art and became a prominent member of the Glasgow School. She designed jewellery and silverwork for Liberty's Cymric range, and also textiles.

ARCHIBALD KNOX (1864–1933)

Born in Cronkbourne on the Isle of Man, Knox, the principal silver and pewter designer for Liberty & Co, created Celtic designs of the highest quality for the Cymric and Tudric schemes. He had previously worked for the Silver Studio (qv) and for Christopher Dresser's Design Studio in Barnes, south-west London, and had taught design at the Wimbledon and Kingston-on-Thames School of Art. At Kingston his teaching methods were considered too unorthodox by the South Kensington Examiners and he resigned his post in 1911.

A description of Knox's new Celtic range from a Liberty catalogue of 1899–1900 shows how keen Arthur Liberty was to promote his work:

> The especially interesting feature ... is its complete and unmistakable differentiation from all other descriptions of modern silverwork. The suggestion, as it were, having its origin in the work of a far earlier period than the greater part of the gold and silver plate ornaments to be found even in the Royal Collections today, the bulk of which only dates back to the Restoration. Cymric silver, although original and initiatory of a new school of work, is suggestive of a more remote era than this, and simplicity is the keynote of its design ...

After 1912, when Knox ceased to work for Liberty's, he went to America where he designed carpets for Bromley & Co of Philadelphia.

MAX LÄUGER (1864–?)

German architect, engineer, sculptor and artist potter chiefly known for his glazed bowls, vases, wall plaques and jugs in stylized Art Nouveau designs. Liberty & Co were the first to import Max Läuger's pottery into the country in the late 1890s. Mark: M.K.L. in monogram with arms of the Grand Duchy of Baden.

W. R. LETHABY (1857–1911)

English architect, metalworker, furniture and pottery designer, Lethaby was also a founder member, in 1884, of the Art Workers' Guild, and Professor of Design at the Royal College of Art in 1900. He designed simple, unpolished furniture, primarily in oak, sometimes in rosewood, and some of it decorated with floral marquetry in ebony, sycamore and bleached mahogany. He also designed fabrics for Liberty & Co in the 1890s.

ERNEST LÉVEILLÉ (flourished 1885–1900)

French Art Nouveau glass designer. Pupil of E. Rousseau with whom he produced experimental glass including many pieces of sculptured crackle glass sold by Liberty & Co at the close of the nineteenth century. Mark: E. Léveillé over E. Rousseau.

SIDNEY MAWSON (c1876–c1937/8)

A textile designer for Liberty & Co in the first decade of the present century.

FRANK MILES (1852–91)

Miles was a textile designer for Liberty & Co in the late 1880s and 1890s when, possibly to meet the competition of Morris & Co, Liberty began to commission work from leading artists and designers of the period.

HARRY NAPPER (1860–1930)

Textile, furniture and metalwork designer with the Silver Studio (*c* 1893–8), Napper provided Liberty & Co with many of their finest fabric designs. He managed the design production of the Silver Studio after Arthur Silver's death in 1896. Mario Amaya (see Bibliography) wrote: 'Around 1900 the strongest personality at Liberty's appears to have been Harry Napper whose fabrics depended less on undulating curves than drifting geometrized motifs, strident with angular petals and thorny leaves.'

JOHN PEARSON (flourished 1890–1910)

A designer and metalworker whose imagery was often fantastic and highly original. Pearson was the first instructor in metalwork at C.R.Ashbee's Guild of Handicrafts and was dismissed in 1890 because 'Mr Pearson had been outside the Guild supplying Messrs Morris and others with goods . . .' He was reinstated but again failed to honour his undertaking not to deal with other firms, and was allowed to resign on 29 August 1892. Thereafter he worked for William Morris and later at the Newlyn Class in Cornwall. Although there is no conclusive documentary evidence that Pearson worked for Liberty & Co, there is some circumstantial evidence that he did supply Liberty with designs. If one compares the copper charger designed and signed by Pearson (see below) with similar designs by J.D. Mackenzie of the Newlyn Class the cross-fertilization of influence is clear.

Charger in repoussé copper by John Pearson, Signed by the artist in engraved script: 'J.P' and dated 1902. Depth 21 in. Sold by Liberty & Co.

E. G. PUNNETT (flourished 1900)

A furniture designer known to have worked for Liberty & Co from the fact that he joined William Birch of High Wycombe in 1901 (*qv*). This firm supplied Liberty with a great deal of furniture and many of their surviving pieces bear Punnett's signature.

E. G. REUTER (1845–after 1912)

A designer of fabrics for Liberty & Co in the 1890s. In his book *The Designs of Archibald Knox for Liberty & Co*, Adrian Tilbrook wrote: 'Liberty and Co were regular exhibitors in the various Arts and Crafts Society Exhibitions beginning with a stand at the New Gallery [Regent Street] in 1893. The company exhibited a large selection of fabrics designed by Arthur Silver, Thomas Wardle, E. G. Reuter and W. R. Lethaby. It is from this source [i.e. exhibitions], and not the company that the names of the various designers were made known.'

RICHARD REIMERSCHMID (1868–1957)

A furniture designer whose work was imported by Liberty & Co in the 1900s, Reimerschmid first became generally known after his participation in the Paris Exhibition of 1900.

J. SCARRATT-RIGBY

Provided Liberty & Co with textile designs in stylized floral patterns in the late 1880s.

ARTHUR SILVER (1853–1896)

Designer and craftsman, founder of the Silver Studio in 1880 and father of Reginald 'Rex' Silver and Harry Silver (*qv*). The Silver Studio specialized in every aspect of design, from plasterwork, metalwork, furniture and book jackets to the design of complete interiors, and they provided Liberty & Co with a great number of fabric designs.

HARRY SILVER (1882–1972)

Metalwork and textile designer with his father's studio (see above). Influenced by Archibald Knox, he executed designs for Liberty Cymric silver after 1906, and supervised the design production of the Silver Studio from 1901 to 1916, when he joined the army.

REGINALD 'REX' SILVER (1879–1965)

The son of Arthur Silver and the brother of Harry (see above), he administered the Silver Studio from 1901 until its closure in 1963. Regarding his association with Liberty & Co and his work in general, see pp. 77–8.

DAVID VEAZEY

Liberty & Co are known to have put into production at least one design by David Veazey: the winning design for a silver tea caddy in a competition organized by Liberty through *The Studio* magazine in 1899. It was produced both in silver and, later, in pewter, bearing the number 049c. The signature used by the artist on this occasion was 'Tramp'.

C. F. A. VOYSEY (1857–1941)

An English architect and designer of furniture, textiles, carpets, tapestries, wallpapers, ceramics and metalwork. His furniture was generally austere and architectural, using straight lines and very little ornament except for a characteristic pierced heart shape, and other cut-out motifs, in the backs of chairs. He produced many textile and wallpaper designs for Liberty & Co between 1890 and 1910. Charles Voysey and George Walton (*qv*) were among a distinguished group of furniture designers who worked directly for Liberty or were influenced by the aesthetic charisma of Leonard Wyburd's design studio (*qv*), itself a centre of highly advanced design in its day. There is often a problem of positive identification: many Voysey designs are typical of the Liberty Style, though they do not always carry the Liberty mark.

GEORGE WALTON (1867–1933)

Scottish architect and designer and a member of the Glasgow School, he collaborated with C.R.Mackintosh on the Cranston Tea Rooms, Glasgow, in 1897. Walton was closely associated with the Arts and Crafts Movement, and worked as a furniture designer for Liberty & Co in the late 1890s and early 1900s.

LEONARD F. WYBURD

Although Leonard Wyburd set up the Liberty Furnishing and Decoration Studio as early as 1883, at the height of the Aesthetic Movement, it was not until the late 1890s that he began to design the avant-garde furniture which was to help revolutionize the whole concept of furniture design, not only in England but also in Vienna, Berlin and Paris (where in 1889 Liberty opened a branch, at 38 Avenue de l'Opéra). Leonard Wyburd is as much a part of the creation of the Liberty Style as is Archibald Knox.

Oak chair from bedroom suite *c*1904. A simple geometric form with marquetry panels of swans in stained fruit woods. Wyburd Studios.

Bibliography

Alison Adburgham, *Liberty's: A Biography of a Shop*, Allen & Unwin, London, 1975.

Mario Amaya, *Art Nouveau*, Studio Vista, London, 1966.

A.H. Barr, *Picasso, Fifty Years of his Art*, Museum of Modern Art, New York, 1946.

Martin Battersby, *The Decorative Twenties*, Studio Vista, London, 1969.
   Art Nouveau, Hamlyn, London, 1969.

Roger Billcliffe, *Charles Rennie Mackintosh*, Lutterworth Press, London, 1979.

Brigid Brophy, *Beardsley and his World*, Thames & Hudson, London, 1976.

A.W. Coysh, *British Art Pottery, 1870–1940*, David & Charles, Newton Abbot, 1976.

Philippe Garner, *Art Nouveau for Collectors*, Hamlyn, London, 1974.

William Gaunt, *The Observer's Book of Modern Art*, Frederick Warne, London, 1964.

Geoffrey A. Godden, *Encyclopaedia of British Pottery and Porcelain Marks*, Barrie and Jenkins, London, 1968.

Philippe Jullian, *Dreamers of Decadence*, Phaidon, London, 1971.

Dan Klein, *Art Deco*, Octopus Books, London, 1974.

Gerald and Celia Larner, *The Glasgow Style*, Astragal Books, London, 1980.

Mervyn Levy, *The Pocket Dictionary of Art Terms*, Long Acre Press, London, 1961.

James Mackay, *Dictionary of Turn of the Century Antiques*, Ward Lock, London, 1974.

Jiri Mucha, *Alphonse Mucha*, Academy Editions, London, 1976.

Gillian Naylor, *The Arts and Crafts Movement*, Studio Vista, London, 1971.

Nicholas Powell, *The Sacred Spring: The Arts in Vienna 1898–1918*, Studio Vista, London, 1974.

Herbert Read, *The Meaning of Art*, Faber & Faber, London, 1931.

Denys Sutton, *Nocturne, The Art of James McNeill Whistler*, Country Life, London, 1963.

Adrian J. Tilbrook, *The Designs of Archibald Knox for Liberty & Co*, Ornament Press, London, 1976.

S. Tschudi Madsen, *Art Nouveau*, Weidenfeld and Nicolson, London, 1967.

Geoffrey Warren, *Art Nouveau*, Octopus Books, London, 1972.

The Collector's Encyclopedia, Victoriana to Art Deco, William Collins, London and Glasgow, 1974.

Foundations of Modern Art: Ozenfant, Dover Publications, London, 1952.

Phaidon Dictionary of Twentieth Century Art, Phaidon Press, London, 1973.

Jessie M. King and E. A. Taylor, Paul Harris Publishing and Sotheby's Belgravia, London, 1977.

Articles and pamphlets

Arthur Lasenby Liberty: *Pewter and the Revival of its use.* Address before the Applied Art Section of the Society for the Encouragement of Arts, Manufacturer and Commerce, London, May, 1904. (Journal of the Society of Arts, 10 June 1904).

Arthur Lasenby Liberty: *Spitalfields Brocades.* First issue of *The Studio* magazine, 1893.
Mario Amaya: *Liberty and the Modern Style, Apollo*, February 1963.
James Laver: *The Liberty Story.* Pamphlet published by Liberty & Co, 1959.

Exhibition Catalogues

Liberty's 1875–1975: an Exhibition to mark the firm's centenary. Victoria and Albert Museum, July–October 1975.
The Aesthetic Movement and the Art of Japan: Fine Art Society London Ltd, 3–27 October 1972.
Birmingham Gold and Silver 1773–1973: City Museum and Art Gallery, Birmingham, 28 July–16 September 1973.
The Arts & Crafts Movement 1890–1930: Fine Art Society London Ltd, 2–27 October 1973.
Christopher Dresser: Fine Art Society London Ltd, 3–27 October 1972.
William Moorcroft and Walter Moorcroft: Richard Dennis, 148 New Bond Street, London, 4–15 December 1973.
Charles Rennie Mackintosh: Victoria & Albert Museum, London, 30 October–29 December 1968.
C.F.A. Voysey, Architect and Designer: Art Gallery and Museums and the Royal Pavilion, Brighton, 11 July–3 September 1978.
Aspects of the Aesthetic Movement: Dan Klein Ltd, London, 5 December–22 December 1978.
A London Design Studio, 1880–1963 – The Silver Studio Collection: Museum of London, 21 November 1980–31 January 1981.
Art Nouveau: Piccadilly Gallery, London, 1965.
Vienna Secession: Royal Academy of Arts, 9 January–7 March 1971.

Index